JOURNAL FOR THE STUDY OF THE OLD TESTAMENT SUPPLEMENT SERIES
82

Editors
David J.A. Clines
Philip R. Davies

BIBLE AND LITERATURE SERIES
26

Almond Press
Sheffield

We dedicate this book to our teachers of long ago

James Muilenburg
and
E.A. Speiser

RHETORIC
and
BIBLICAL
INTERPRETATION

Dale Patrick
and
Allen Scult

The Almond Press · 1990

Bible and Literature Series, 26

General Editor: David M. Gunn
(Columbia Theological Seminary, Decatur, Georgia)
Assistant General Editor: Danna Nolan Fewell
(Perkins School of Theology, Dallas, Texas)
Consultant Editors: Elizabeth Struthers Malbon
(Virginia Polytechnic Institute & State University, Blacksburg, Virginia)
James G. Williams
(Syracuse University, Syracuse, New York)

Published by Almond Press

Editorial direction: David M. Gunn
Columbia Theological Seminary
P.O. Box 520, Decatur
GA 30031, U.S.A.

Almond Press is an imprint of
Sheffield Academic Press Ltd
The University of Sheffield
343 Fulwood Road
Sheffield S10 3BP
England

Typeset by Sheffield Academic Press and
Printed in Great Britain
by Billing & Sons Ltd
Worcester

British Library Cataloguing in Publication Data

Patrick, Dale
    Rhetoric and biblical interpretation.
    1. Bible—Critical studies
    I. Title   II. Scult, Allen   III. Series
    220.6

ISSN 0260-4493
ISSN 0309-0787
ISBN 1-85075-222-2

CONTENTS

Preface   7

Part I

Chapter 1
RHETORICAL CRITICISM AND BIBLICAL EXEGESIS   11

Chapter 2
THE RHETORICAL CHARACTER OF BIBLICAL
NARRATIVE   29

Chapter 3
A RHETORICAL VIEW OF HISTORICAL NARRATIVE   45

Chapter 4
FORENSIC NARRATION IN BIBLICAL NARRATIVE   57

Part II

Chapter 5
FINDING THE BEST JOB   81

Chapter 6
GENESIS AND POWER   103

Chapter 7
'THE BIBLE SAYS. . .'   127

Notes   141
Select Bibliography   161
Index of Biblical References   165
Index of Authors   167
Index of Subjects   169

PREFACE

This book grows out of a number of years of conversation about rhetoric and Biblical interpretation. Perhaps because one of us is a rhetorician by trade, we became conscious of the fact that as the content of our thought together began to take shape, so did our manner of conversing about it. Indeed, because a conversation also involves continual interpretation of one another's comments, we sometimes found ourselves drawn into talk about these interpretations, and then applying the understandings gleaned from such 'meta-talk' to an exploration of our interpretative relationship to the text. Because this web of hermeneutical connections affects the outcome of such collaborative efforts in interpretation, leading also to some knotty problems of 'voice'—whether to speak as one or as two (a bit like some of the problems our authors might have faced!)—we felt some comments about our conversation were in order, so that the reader might have an idea of 'who's who and what's what' in the pages which follow.

Our conversation began, as most do perhaps, with each of us offering tentative pieces of our own perspective for the other's consideration. As we came to know each other, these offerings also began to assimilate some of the other's language, by way of building common ground. Such linguistic common ground enabled us better to explore a position together, from multiple perspectives, and thereby to think through its possibilities more fully. This joining of intellectual forces in the exploration of different positions and perhaps eventually in the formation of a common one is suggested by Hans Georg Gadamer as a much preferred hermeneutical alternative to the usual scholarly dialectic of hard position taking, followed by attack and defense.[1] We never explicitly agreed to avoid such hard position taking. We just seemed to have eased into the hermeneutical

alternative—the mutual exploration of the possible rightness of different positions, no matter who offered them—as a more pleasant mode of discoursing together.

This step was probably facilitated by a happy historical accident: We each had been moving along lines which were ready to converge with the other. Indeed, each seemed in need of the other's line of thinking in order to advance. Patrick had been reflecting on the possibilities of the rhetorical perspective. His ideas grew out of form criticism, especially as practiced by his early teacher, James Muilenburg. But rhetorical criticism, as it developed from Muilenburg's ideas and those of his students, did not quite add up to a fully developed method of interpretation which integrated the language of the text itself with its subsequent effect on audiences. What was needed was a fuller understanding of rhetoric as the way a text manages its relationship with its audiences—an understanding which grows out of the ancient and modern traditions of rhetoric and hermeneutics.

Scult's rhetorical perspective on the Bible, in addition to being informed by his own disciplinary background in rhetoric and hermeneutics, also benefited from the rhetorically sensitive approach of his early teacher in Bible, E.A. Speiser, and was sparked later by his reading of James Muilenburg's Presidential Address to the Society for Biblical Literature, 'Form Criticism and Beyond'.[2] But he was lacking a thorough acquaintance with the scholarly traditions of Biblical study and their methods of interpretation. Thus each of us had both a predisposition to find common ground with the other, and a need for the knowledge the other would bring to the building of that common ground. We hope we managed the integration of our different disciplinary traditions well, such that the rhetorical perspective elaborated in Chapter 1 represents not only a good mix, but an appropriate 'moving beyond'.

The conversation, of which this book is a part, began long before we thought of writing the book and will probably continue long after. At a certain point, we seemed to have inadvertently stumbled upon what seemed like a good starting point for developing a rhetorical method of interpretation and applying it. So we started writing, as well as talking. While the only chapter actually written together from scratch is Chapter 1, elaborating our method, the other pieces were brought into the mutuality of the conversation using much the same 'computer-assisted' approach: We would submit each essay on 'disc' to the other for editing and rewriting. Before examining each set of

emendations, the original essay and the changes would be fully
discussed by way of arriving at a common conceptualization from
which to rewrite the whole. So in every case, the authorial 'we' you
see in the text represents a very real blend of traditions, perspectives,
and finally even each other's written material, into a new whole text,
reconceptualized through our conversation together. However, our
first thought was still to maintain the first person in the individual
chapters because that seemed to more honestly reflect the original
process of composition. But when we read through the book, the 'I's'
not only grated because of the incongruence with the professed dual
authorship, but also because the 'I's' did not take account of a rather
difficult struggle at creating an integrated text. So we finally decided
to present the text to you, in its entirety, as an imperfect 'ours', for in
point of fact, we endeavored to make it one text, and so feel it should
be read and judged as such. In this regard, we should also note that
the authors share equal responsibility for what follows.

Dale Patrick
Allen Scult

Introductory Note
The authors wish to inform their American readers that the British
convention of single rather than double quotation marks has been
adopted throughout the text. Unless otherwise noted all translations
of Biblical passages are from the *Tanakh* of the Jewish Publication
Society (Philadelphia, 1985).

PART I

Chapter 1

RHETORICAL CRITICISM AND BIBLICAL EXEGESIS

The current importance of rhetorical criticism in Biblical studies can be traced to James Muilenburg's Presidential Address to the Society of Biblical Literature in 1968. This speech, entitled 'Form Criticism and Beyond',[1] was something of a departing charge to his colleagues and students. His exegetical work and reflection had convinced him that form criticism was on the verge of becoming scholastic, and needed to be transcended. He had his idea of how this could be accomplished, but he knew that his creative years were waning. So, in this speech, he bequeathed the task to the coming generation.

Muilenburg's essential complaint against form criticism was its reduction of Biblical passages to 'stereotyped' language. The individuality and uniqueness of each passage were seen simply as variations of genres, fixed by tradition: Reports of personal revelations were categorized as repeated liturgies; thundering commands, shattering judgments, and rousing promises became cultic formulas in a self-enclosed liturgical drama. The words referred to nothing outside the walls of the sanctuary.

Although this accusation did not fit all form critics equally well, there was a marked tendency for the methodology to eclipse the individual passage by focusing on generic components which the passage shared with others. The individual passage became rationally explicable and 'real' only by virtue of its identifiable generic qualities. Against this version of an ancient realism, Muilenburg countered:

> For after all has been said and done about the forms and types of biblical speech, there still remains the task of discerning the actuality of the particular text, and it is with this... that we must reckon..., for it is this concreteness which marks the material with which we are dealing.[2]

To recover the particular text, Muilenburg called for a revival of an older form of analysis, frequently termed 'stylistic criticism'. He proposed the new name 'rhetorical criticism' and it stuck. The objective of this type of analysis was the delineation of independent textual units (or pericopes) and their internal structure: 'Persistent and painstaking attention to the modes of Hebrew literary composition will reveal that the pericopes exhibit linguistic patterns, word formations ordered and arranged in particular ways, verbal sequences which move in fixed structures from beginning to end'.[3]

Although in the hands of Muilenburg's followers, the method has yielded bold, sophisticated attempts to interpret texts by attending to their rhetorical shape, it has still failed to live up to Muilenburg's call to encounter texts in their concrete particularity. This failure correlates with the limitation of rhetorical criticism in Biblical studies to stylistic analysis. We believe rhetorical criticism does indeed hold the key to realizing Muilenburg's vision, but not if it is unnecessarily confined to an analysis of stylistic devices.

In order to lead to a deeper penetration into the particularity and concreteness of the text, the 'rhetoric' in rhetorical criticism must be broadened to its fullest range in the classical tradition, namely, *as the means by which a text establishes and manages its relationship to its audience in order to achieve a particular effect.*[4] This, of course, includes stylistic devices, but goes beyond style to encompass the whole range of linguistic instrumentalities by which a discourse constructs a particular relationship with an audience in order to communicate a message.

Additionally, there is a strong suggestion in classical rhetoric, especially in Aristotle, that 'true rhetoric', the construction of the 'right' relationship with an audience, holds epistemic possibilities— that indeed knowledge grows out of a particular way of speaking. Hence Aristotle opens his treatise on rhetoric with the statement, 'Rhetoric is the counterpart of dialectic', thus claiming that rhetoric is a legitimate philosophical enterprise.[5] A number of contemporary philosophers, most notably Hans Georg Gadamer and Richard Rorty,[6] have joined rhetorical scholars[7] in pursuing the possibilities of rhetoric as a way of knowing.[8]

Of course, the Biblical authors were not acquainted with the classical view of rhetoric, let alone Aristotle's attempt to make it into a legitimate way of doing philosophy. So at this point our readers might well accuse us of pushing this view of Biblical rhetoric too far and counsel us to return to the more limited focus of rhetorical

criticism on elements of Biblical style. We would respond, echoing
the literary critic, Kenneth Burke, that the use of rhetoric, in this
broader sense, is no more dependent on one's acquaintance with
classical texts on the subject, than is one's use of stylistic devices.[9]
Rhetoric, in both senses, is an inherent function of language use: Any
author must necessarily shape his or her language in one way rather
than another, and insofar as we may assume artful deliberateness on
the author's part, the shape and form of the discourse is an indication
of how he or she means for us to take the message. It is thus through
a text's rhetoric that a modern interpreter can recapture the
possibilities for encounter the particular text holds.

Now it is unlikely that either Muilenburg or most of his students
were very much aware of this dimension of the classical concept of
rhetoric, or of its revival in contemporary rhetorical theory and
criticism, and so their tendency to limit rhetoric to stylistics is
perfectly understandable. But we find it significant that even though
there are no overt references to the classical dimension of the concept
in Muilenburg's address, we see in it a strong urge to follow the text
back to its original transaction with an audience.[10] This suggests
Muilenburg understood the importance of sensitivity to the rhetorically
constructed speaker–audience relationship for enacting his vision of
rediscovering the living particularity of the text; he simply did not
have the disciplinary language to express it.

In the pages which follow we propose to draw out those elements
in Muilenburg's vision which point toward this broader notion of
rhetorical criticism and then, using insights from the rhetorical
tradition, to outline a method of doing rhetorical criticism which we
believe is a fitting response to Muilenburg's charge: namely, to move
beyond the mere identification of forms and genres towards
reconstituting the text as a piece of living discourse. In developing
our ideas in this way, we hope to show that our rhetorical approach
to Biblical exegesis is a legitimate integration of rhetoric and Biblical
studies, bearing a logical connection to each method of analysis. We
begin the 'archaeological' portion of our task by exploring the roots of
the rhetorical approach in Muilenburg's critique of form criticism.

The Development of the Rhetorical Perspective

Any method of interpretation represents an attempt to reconstruct
the situation in which the interpreter must place him- or herself in
order to understand the text properly. Form criticism can be seen as

growing out of a perceived inadequacy in this 'hermeneutical situation' as constructed by source criticism. On the surface, this inadequacy was described as the neglect of the oral phase of transmission. But even the connotation of the central form critical concept, *Sitz im Leben*, suggests that form critics were after something more than just the text's original oral form: They sought to rediscover the text as a living thing. They appear to have adopted the distinctly rhetorical view that a text 'lives' in relationship to an audience. This is evidenced by their effort to delineate, in as much detail as possible, the 'occasion' on which the text was presented orally to an audience. There is an immediacy of impact or effect that a speaker must somehow produce in the transaction with his audience in order for his speech to 'work'. This immediacy in the speaker–audience relationship is the soul of oral discourse, and form critics tried to exhume that soul by reconstructing the occasion.

However, the problem, as Muilenburg observed, was that the attempt to reconstruct occasions through the analysis of forms became a search for the 'typical and the representative'.[11] Thus, their scholarly proclivity to systematize and generalize led form critics to lose sight of the identification of forms as merely an *instrument*, whose purpose it was to illuminate the unique life of a particular pericope. The identification of forms and occasions became an end in itself and the original insight, that orality was the key to unlocking the rhetorical life of the text, was lost.

There are other hints that the rhetorical process was actually at the heart of the form critical project, especially in Muilenburg's view of it. Perhaps the most significant is the way form critics look at genre: namely, as the form discourse takes in order to serve a particular *function* in the community.[12] This notion of genre suggests that the way the discourse was meant to function for the audience is available to us in the original form or shape into which the discourse was put. Thus, tracing the text back to those original forms is a way for the interpreter to rediscover the discourse as it might have existed in the life of the community.

Unfortunately, the methodological imperative again overpowered the insight. The correlation of form and function became an end in itself, rather than a means to understanding the way the utterance engages its audience. In the process, the concept of function was frequently narrowed to ritual function, for that was easiest to support, and then to generalize to other passages.[13]

The idea that the form or shape of a discourse is the key to how it

functions for an audience is basic to the rhetorical perspective. But in the rhetorical perspective, function is seen more broadly: It refers to how a discourse is meant to act upon, or affect an audience. Through the shape into which speakers cast their message they tell the audience how they mean it to be engaged and therefore to be understood. Of course, the auditors are free to interpret the language of the discourse in any way they wish, but the speaker or author attempts to constrain that freedom and direct interpretation by giving the audience cues and indicators as to how he or she means the discourse to function for them.

These cues or indicators are communicated through the speaker's management of the conventional forms of discourse prevalent in the community to which speaker and audience belong. In cases where authority is exercised, for example, the effective employment of the appropriate form gives the utterance its binding force. Thus in order for the critic to comprehend the nature of a text's authority fully in this case, he or she needs to find those conventions of engagement through which the text might have originally exercised its authority over an audience. From a rhetorical perspective, then, a text's genre becomes the code that must be broken in order to bring its word to life.

In this regard as well, Muilenburg's prescience about the unrealized possibilities of form criticism points the way. After observing that 'The propensity of form critics to pay exclusive attention to the *Gattung* may actually obscure the thought and intention of the writer or speaker', he argues that 'form and content are inextricably related'.[14] If we understand content as a message communicated through persuasion and power relations, the 'form' holds the key to content. The generic features of the form use the conventions of the community to engender the engagement necessary for the text to communicate its meaning. The form, thus, does not simply indicate an 'outward' occasion, but points 'inward' to the very meaning of the text.

If form is not to be reduced to genre, but is a particular and possibly unique realization of a community's conventions of engagement in a specific text, Muilenburg was quite correct to fault form critics for their failure to 'supplement [their] form critical analysis with a careful inspection of the literary unit in its precise and unique formulation'.[15] Again, he is suggesting that the form should be a way *into* an encounter with the particular passage in all its uniqueness, rather than an end in itself. If the introduction of the word

'encounter' here seems a bit too existential for a scholar of
Muilenburg's sensibilities, note his characterization of Gunkel as an
interpreter and teacher:

> It is not too much to say that Gunkel has never been excelled in his
> ability to portray the spirit which animated the Biblical writers,
> and he did not hesitate either in his lectures or in his seminars to
> draw upon the events of contemporary history or the experiences of
> the common man to explicate the meaning of a pericope.[16]

Thus when he wishes to characterize Gunkel's talent and skill as a
form critic, Muilenburg strongly suggests that it was his capacity to
use the form to see into what the Biblical writers were trying to say
and then to find ways to share his insight with his students by
bringing their 'life situation' to bear so they might encounter the text
more personally ('across horizons', to use contemporary hermeneutical
parlance).

Here Muilenburg's words hint at yet another significant aspect of
the rhetorical perspective: the nature of discourse as 'addressed'.[17]
Rhetoric is that quality of discourse which does not allow it to 'stand
still'; rather, it gives the discourse a voice which moves outward and
gives it the capacity to address audiences, both immediate and more
distant in time and place. Thus, in order to interpret an ancient text,
the interpreter must first reconstruct the discourse's mode of address
and permit him- or herself to be addressed by it, and then transmit
that mode of address to his or her contemporary audience. The
interpreter must, in effect, re-invent and 'speak' the text's message to
his or her contemporary audience in a way that carries the addressed
message of the text, in a genuine and faithful manner, one step
further. Gadamer, echoing this notion of rhetoric as the 'addressed'
quality of discourse, refers to this process of inventing and speaking a
text's message anew as the rhetorical dimension of hermeneutical
activity.[18]

However powerful these intimations we have explored, Muilenburg's
concrete suggestions regarding how to supplement form criticism
addressed only one of its deficiencies: its propensity for generality. In
response, he proposed a method for grasping the particular, unique
form of a given text. The teacher of literature in him won out; he
revived style criticism under the conviction that close attention to
the artistic devices of composition would lead the interpreter to the
content of what the author had to say.

But there was an incipient ambiguity in this methodology which

arises from the composite character of many Biblical passages. When the text shows evidence of having been assembled from more than one utterance or constructed from pieces of several sources, is the interpreter to search for the form of the constituent parts or that of the received text? Muilenburg would probably have opted for the original utterance or writing, for he was enamored of source and form criticism.[19] He desired to supplement and correct the over-refinement of these methods, not contest their hermeneutical claims.

His students, however, soon discovered that the rhetorical patterns of the text could frequently be traced across divisions drawn by source and form criticism. A new hermeneutic emerged from this discovery: Interpretation should be of the extant text, not of hypothetical reconstructions of the originals. This turn toward the text as we have received it has become axiomatic not only for rhetorical criticism, but for all types of scholarship which seek out the artistic qualities of the text.[20]

The principle of the extant text was both refreshing and cogent. The text, as we have it, does, after all, communicate powerfully. Yet, source, form and traditio-historical criticism have frequently obscured its capacity to do so. The critical scholar has been so thoroughly trained to look for seams and discrepancies that it is often difficult to make sense of a passage until it has been 'deconstructed'. The time was ripe for scholarship to seek to interpret the text that Jews and Christians, and non-believers as well, have been reading for more than 2000 years.[21]

Unfortunately, as part of their attempt to recover and legitimize the extant text, rhetorical and literary critics lost touch with the insights into the pre-canonical exchanges with audiences that had been identified and studied by source, form and traditio-historical critics. Additionally, the shift of focus to the extant text also appears to have cost rhetorical critics their sense for the active part played by the audience (including the interpreter) in the creation of meaning. The rhetorical or artistic design of the text seems to have been isolated by these critics as an object of contemplation and appreciation in its own right. The text is regarded as a literary artifact whose effect can be explained solely by reference to the elegance of its artistry.

It is not accidental that rhetorical critics and the first wave of literary critics were attracted to the literary critical school known as 'New Criticism'.[22] Like practitioners of the new criticism, rhetorical critics of the Old Testament, and some of the literary critics who

made common cause with them, divorced form from its service to content and effect on the audience. Perhaps they needed to have taken more seriously Muilenburg's observation that form and content are 'inextricably related', and recognized that the artistic embellishment of a text serves its *communicative* purpose.

This is not to say that the exploration of the artistic features of Old Testament narrative and poetry has been without merit; to the contrary, it is today the most exciting field of Biblical studies. Robert Alter, in his seminal work on the Bible's narrative art,[23] did much to teach the community of Biblical scholars about this connection between art and communication; and his colleagues in literature, that the Bible should be taken seriously as a work of literary art. His emphasis, therefore, was understandably on the similarities the Bible shares with other great literary works. Thus he makes a powerful and detailed argument for reading the Biblical narratives as attempts on the part of the authors to discover and communicate through their art 'what it is like to be a human being'.[24] As a result of Alter's work, the interpreter may confidently assume artistic deliberateness on the part of the Biblical authors and use the artfulness of the narratives as a conduit to the author's worldview just as he or she would any great work of literature. In short, Alter gives the Biblical narrators the credibility to speak to an audience through their narrative art.

While this approach also strongly intimates the rhetorical approach we have been tracing, it falls short of bringing the interpreter into a full-bodied encounter with the Biblical text, for the Bible is obviously not just a great work of literature, but also claims to embody a great spiritual vision. We therefore maintain that, as difficult as it might be to do so without losing scholarly objectivity, the interpreter must somehow engage the spiritual and theological truth claims of the Biblical text in order to understand it rightly. A rhetorical perspective must recognize the artful form—the rhetorical shape—of the Biblical text as the essential vehicle through which its truth claims are communicated. If, for example, we say that certain portions of the Bible are to be generically identified and therefore rightly understood as artful narrative, then their narrative construction becomes the key to fathoming the spiritual or religious argument being made. This step, Alter's scholarly reserve seems to prevent him from taking.

In another recent work, Meir Sternberg[25] also explores the Bible's narrative art, and does so with explicit reference to rhetoric as the means by which the text artfully engages its audience. Sternberg uses his rhetorical insights to find his way to the narrative infrastructure

of the text, showing in minute detail how the text engages the audience step by step in dramatic encounter. But in so doing, Sternberg's project becomes reduced to a virtuoso formalism: The ultimate object of inquiry is still the form and shape on the surface of the text itself. The argument that lies just beneath the surface of these shapes and forms, for which they are vehicles of encounter, becomes lost in the minutiae of Sternberg's analysis. Sternberg's reading of the text is one that only a scholar could manage. He does not use his scholarly sensitivity to the forms and shapes of the text to uncover the life the text might have had within a religious community.

Thus, even the concept of the world-creating power of artistry does not catch the rhetorical force of the Bible's design. For the Biblical text, unlike fiction, does not simply ask for a 'willing suspension of disbelief', in order to temporarily inhabit the world the artist has created. Rather, it seeks to persuade its readers to accept the depicted world as their world. It is the shaping of the text to elicit faith which the rhetorical perspective must engage, and thereby complete the work of literary analysis.

Rhetorical Analysis and Hermeneutics

If a text is a communication between an author and a reader, we cannot avoid the interactive character even of the scholarly reading of the text. The text's meaning is not inherent in its linguistic configuration or its author's intention, but rather in the transaction or conversation between the text and the spiritual seeker addressed by its rhetoric. The scholar must somehow enter into that conversation—must become the text's reader, so to speak.

Such a notion, of course, challenges the model of disinterested scholarship, in which the ideal is to bracket out the interpreter's subjectivity. But it seems to us that the analytical approach to the text inverts the proper relationship between text and reader. If one considers a text as an object, it has nothing to offer the interpreter in the latter's search for meaning. Rather, it is a phenomenon to be 'mastered', by being described, classified and explained. Thus the 'power' in the relationship effectively passes from text to interpreter, and the text's rhetorical capacity to address is lost.

The reader is probably familiar with this critique from the writings and lectures of hermeneutical philosophers.[26] The 'objectivist' model of interpretation has been under attack for some time. Unfortunately,

however, the task of hermeneutical reflection still tends to be assigned to theologians and preachers. Meanwhile, the scholarly community continues to operate with a distinction between 'what a text meant' and 'what it means'. The former is assigned to critical scholarship, the latter to religiously inclined interpreters. This division of labor allows critical scholarship to maintain its pretense of objectivity.

Hermeneutics, however, cannot be separated from a critical approach which also presumes to recognize that meaning grows out of a rhetorical transaction: The text is meaningful only to someone who seeks to understand it as an engaged 'subject'. The problem, of course, is how to manage this engagement and still be faithful to one's critical responsibilities.

It is our belief that the rhetorical perspective can interject hermeneutics into critical interpretation without compromising the rigor of scholarly analysis. The task begins with a reconstruction of the significant interpretive moments in the text's history. Here much of the work has already been done by existing exegetical approaches. These approaches need to be reconceptualized, however, as attempts to recover a moment in the history of a text in which it was a living communication. From this perspective, the limits of each approach are due to the boundaries of the moment it reconstructs. These limits are perhaps most salient in the case of source criticism. While a precise delineation of sources and their dates of composition has revealed significant individual moments of meaning in the text's evolution, the method also loses a sense of the text's earlier oral life and of its later life as an integrated whole. Since the text has lived a succession of significant interpretive moments, each must be seen as contributing to the full meaning of the text, which is contained in its entire history of interpretation. The interpreter, therefore, must synthesize the meanings a text has had into the meaning it has in order to understand it fully.

It must be emphasized at this point that we are not proposing a history of interpretation, but rather a method of interpretation which takes *selective* account of history. All of those historical moments in which a text was meaningful cannot and should not carry equal weight. The interpreter must judge which moments in a text's history constitute the effective movement of meaning from the text to the interpreter.

These moments will most likely be part of the tradition (or traditions) of interpretation in which the interpreter stands, for, in

the final analysis, it is the interpreter's own judgment, made in the context of his or her own historicity, which must ground the interpretation. Thus the interpreter must decide with which other interpreters he or she is making his or her interpretive judgments. This decision is not unlike one we all commonly make—that is, with whom to discuss important matters about which we must make judgments. That decision itself affects the quality of our judgment and is indeed a central part of it. This 'judging with' has been an essential component of the both the Aristotelian and Kantian traditions of interpretive theory from their very beginnings.[27] As Hannah Arendt observes in her discussion of taste, based on Kant, a man of taste is 'one who knows how to choose his company among men, among things, among thoughts, in the present as well as in the past. . .[He] decides not only how the world is to look, but also who belongs together in it'.[28]

The Best Text

The exegetical task is not finished, however, when the text's meanings over time have been surveyed and selectively ordered; the exegete is also called upon to offer an interpretation of his or her own. This interpretation involves a further act of judgment. The exegete must assess the 'fit' of the various moments in interpretive history with the text which engendered those moments. After all, the text is a determinate communication (that is, it says one thing and not another), and so must somehow be privileged by being the norm for assessing its own realizations.

How do we gain access to '*the* text' which functions as the norm of its realizations? We certainly cannot return to original authorial intent or any other model which leaves out its reception by an audience. The rhetorical perspective bids us to locate the normative text somehow in the exchange between it and the exegete. Here we introduce a hermeneutical principle taken from the legal philosopher Ronald Dworkin: Interpret the text as the best text it can be.[29] Such an interpretation measures the different meanings a text has had against the interpreter's judgment as to what the text in its entirety, construed consistently and naturally, taken in its fullest and most profound sense, can communicate.[30]

The judgment as to what reading of the text makes it best involves a decision as to what kind of text it is. We must decide which generic classification fits the entire text with the greatest consistency and the most illuminating possibilities. This generic identification becomes

the working hypothesis for the attempt to make of this the best text it can be. We must not lose sight of the fact that the identification of the text's genre is aimed at understanding it in its particularity. The guiding question is, 'Does interpreting this text as an instantiation of the proposed genre bring out the full range and depth of its meaningfulness as the particular text it is?' This approach is an attempt to reconstitute the process of interpretation as 'a hermeneutical circle': In hermeneutical terms, the generic identification serves as a 'pre-understanding' which guides the interpretation of the particular text, yet may also be changed by it. Thus the identification of the genre is made subservient to the particular text by serving as a critical frame for a committed and involved attempt to make this particular text the best text it can be. This 'experiential testing out' then circles back and serves as the criterion for assessing the validity of the generic identification, thus continuing to privilege the particular text.

The interpreter's judgment throughout this hermeneutical circle is in turn judged through the ability to recreate rhetorically the power of the text to mean as he or she construes it. His or her construal of 'the best text' is not an objective claim based on the hard and sure philological evidence of corroborative texts. Rather, it is a rhetorical claim about the text's appeal, and so must be argued rhetorically from the text itself, through its interpretive traditions to the interpreter's audience. Thus, every act of interpretation is itself a rhetorical act in that it attempts to reconstruct in language for an audience the thought behind the text.

This rhetorical re-enactment of the text's meaning takes place within an interpretive community—a religious community and/or a community of scholars. This community has passed on the knowledge necessary for interpretation and the framework in which it expects the knowledge to be understood. Exegetical work must meet the standards of knowledge and perspective embodied in the community's tradition; it must be framed to persuade the community that the interpretation offered meets these standards.

This communal dimension of the exegete's work can and frequently does circumscribe the freedom of the exegete to pursue new possibilities of understanding. The problem for a rhetorical hermeneutics is how to balance the claims of the community and the freedom of exegetical inquiry. These can be balanced if we adopt the maxim that a text is to be interpreted as the best text it can be. The exegete, then, can aim his or her exegesis at showing the community that

such an interpretation provides it with the best reading of its text. The community can judge whether this interpretation and the reasoning supporting it in fact do so according to its standards for making such judgments.

Negotiating Roles

In the foregoing pages, we have explored the concept of rhetoric for the richness it has to offer Biblical exegesis. We found intimations of that richness in the insights of form criticism, especially as interpreted and critiqued by James Muilenburg. Using the rhetorical tradition to build upon Muilenburg's insights, we showed how the critic can encounter the text as a living discourse by investigating its rhetorical power to address audiences through the ages. We also suggested how the interpreter can responsibly integrate the meanings the text has had with an interpretation of his or her own by making an argument for that interpretation as the best text it can be.

We conclude with an explicit suggestion as to how the interpreter might balance the roles of scholar and religious or spiritual human being in the process of interpretation; for we believe that each of these roles is crucial to a rhetorical analysis of the text.

Despite the obvious difficulties, we see the religious perspective as essential to genuine rhetorical criticism because, as we have suggested, the text is designed to persuade its readers to make particular choices which can only be called religious. The different religious communities which have lived out these choices provide the context for understanding this persuasive thrust. Without a fairly intimate acquaintance with one of these religious traditions, it is difficult for the scholar to have a basis for interpreting a Biblical text as the best religious text it can be. The Bible is not, after all, a philosophical text addressed to the scholar in his or her study, but a religious text addressing the reader as a member of a worshipping community.

But critical scholars can rightly object that the gains that they have made in understanding the Bible and the history it purports to recount depend upon maintaining a critical distance from the text. Historical reason must be left unfettered by religious or ideological commitments in order to discover what can be known *about* the text.

We are in sympathy with this desire to preserve the scholarly distance from the text that has motivated Biblical scholarship from

its inception. But we also share an equally legitimate desire, prevalent in contemporary hermeneutics, to understand the particular text through its rhetorical power to address us personally. The problem, then, is managing these seemingly contradictory impulses— somehow to make them supportive of, rather than antagonistic to one another.

We believe that the rhetorical perspective elaborated in this essay provides a way to balance and integrate the claims of these two aspects of the interpreter's persona.[31] Because the scholar is involved in showing that the text's genre, its rhetorical shape, indicates that it should be engaged in a particular way, his or her encounter with the text becomes the experiential test for a generic claim. The process of interpreting the text as the best text it can be, however, also requires that the interpreter apply the generic hypothesis in a full-bodied, personal encounter with the text as Scripture: In order adequately to test the generic hypothesis using the best test criterion, the scholar must bring out the fullest meaning of the particular scriptural text he or she is working with. Thus, the norms of scholarly discourse provide a basis for managing the spiritual encounter with the text so that, in the hands of a sensitive scholar/interpreter, it yields historical insight as well as personal understanding, observation as well as testimony, judgment as well as conviction. Such a religiously full-bodied, yet critically rigorous approach would be a fitting enactment of Muilenburg's vision of rhetorical criticism.

A Look Ahead

The chapters that follow provide examples of the sorts of questions stimulated by the rhetorical approach we have outlined, the types of reasoning used to answer those questions, and the kinds of exegetical fruits the approach may yield. Each argues a specific thesis which can stand on its own, but the sequence of chapters is also augmentative in that each one shapes a context in which the subsequent chapters may be most profitably read.

The first three chapters, grouped together as Part I, demonstrate how the rhetorical perspective can be used to deal with questions of genre, in this case the definition or classification of Biblical prose narrative. Because these sorts of questions are commonly part of rhetorical criticism, it is perhaps in this section that the distinctiveness of our approach and its responsiveness to Muilenburg's charge to treat texts in their concrete particularity might be most clearly seen.

Our 'best text criterion' is at work behind the scenes here leading us to try to find a way of generically placing the texts which does justice to their concrete particularity while at the same time accounting for their more universal impact, their status as vehicles of enduring truths. Scholars who render a satisfactory account of how the text functioned in the life-situation which gave it its original form only tell part of the story, for the texts before us have had a significant life beyond that original situation. The Biblical texts achieved canonical status not only because they were exemplary representations of certain significant forms of sacred literature and liturgy, but also because they were persuasive enough to be heard as speaking truths beyond their own time and place. An interpretive approach which meets the 'best text' criterion must identify and analyze the text in a way which simultaneously renders a satisfactory account of its timelessness, and at the same time explains the function it had in its original *Sitz im Leben*.

The sequence in the section is from general to specific. Chapter 2 endeavors to show that the Biblical narratives are amenable to rhetorical analysis not only because their transaction with their audience is induced by their figurational shape, but also because that shape has persuasion as its primary objective. It is argued that examining the text as rhetorical or suasory discourse is consonant with the Biblical authors' view of their subject matter, God's actions in history, which themselves have a rhetorical or suasive purpose. This view of the Biblical narratives is further supported by the fact that their earliest post-canonical interpreters, the Rabbis of the Midrash, framed their interpretation as narrative in a similar rhetorical vein, thus continuing the influence of what was perceived to be the divine rhetorical impulse.

Chapter 3 narrows the scope of prose narratives under consideration to those which rehearse the history of Israel. The question here is whether these narratives should be classified as history, or as realistic fiction, and, if history, in what sense. After a discussion of the significant differences between the two as regards the reading of the Biblical narratives, it is argued that they were meant to be read as a particular sort of corporate history, whose 'truth' lies not in facticity *per se*, but in a faithful rendering of the community's identity. This rendering is accomplished rhetorically by the narratives' making a compelling case that they embody the community's true destiny.

But this rhetorical definition of history still leaves the question of

its facticity unsettled and the specific rhetorical purpose of any given narrative open. Chapter 4 seeks to answer these questions for one set of historical narratives, passages which narrate events in such a way as to persuade the reader of the guilt or innocence of the parties involved. This sort of story, which we can call 'forensic narration', builds a persuasive account around publicly known facts, filling in gaps and probing motives to convict the guilty and exonerate the innocent.

The chapters in Part I address questions which have been on the agenda of critical Biblical scholarship for some time. We merely extend established scholarly methodologies to account for the generative transactions between text and audience. The response of subsequent audiences is secondary here, used to support the reconstruction of the response of the original audience or to exemplify the way a text might continue to communicate after its original context has passed.

The chapters in Part II turn from the focus on the original transaction to the history of interpretation. Here we are seeking a means for both appreciating and adjudicating the diverse meanings passages have had for different times, communities, and individual interpreters. There is a dialectic at the center of the rhetorical conception of textual meaning. If a text has meaning, i.e., communicates a message, in a transaction with its audience, then every transaction— every time a text has become *effective* for an audience—constitutes a part of its meaning. In other words, a text means all that it has meant. On the other hand, the interpreter must take a position on the text's determinate meaning—make a judgment about what the text means in the present in the light of all the knowledge and wisdom he or she possesses. This requires a means of adjudicating interpretations, formulating one's own, and arguing for its legitimacy.

As we have already indicated, we propose as a guiding principle for assessing and adjudicating interpretations the dictum: Interpret a text as the best text it can be. This principle was in the background of the chapters of Part I dealing with genre: Each classification claims to construe Biblical prose narratives as the way to read them so that they communicate their truth most effectively. In Part II the principle is in the foreground: It is used to develop a way of reading a text which resolves the significant problems and conflicts in its interpretive history and enables it to communicate its meaning most effectively.

Chapter 5 defines the dictum that one interpret a text as the best text it can be, establishes criteria for assessing whether an interpretation does so, and argues for the adoption of this principle. To demonstrate its usefulness, the chapter then applies it to a variety of problems confronting the interpreter of Job. In the course of this demonstration, many scholarly proposals regarding translation, sources, genre and sequentiality are evaluated against this fundamental principle of interpretation.

Chapter 6 is a reading of Genesis 1–3. Its exegetical focus is on the juxtaposition of the two accounts of creation. It argues for a 'best text' reading of these two accounts first separately, then together as a discourse on power. When they are read in this way, the compelling force of these accounts is shown to be a function both of their accurate rendering of the nature of power and of their character as archetypical examples of how power may be constituted by discourse.

Chapter 7 takes the question of synthesis to its highest level, that of the Old Testament as a whole. The chapter addresses the issue debated among Biblical interpreters whether or not the writings of the OT are too diverse to be synthesized into one unitary theological scheme. It is argued that the text is shaped to be read synthetically, ultimately because the oneness of the Biblical God requires it. The reader who is committed to reading the text as the best text it can be will take up the task of completing the synthesis inaugurated by the text.

The six chapters as a whole only begin to explore the possibilities in the rhetorical approach so imaginatively presaged by James Muilenburg. In some cases, scholarly theses with some currency will be reinforced by being examined rhetorically. In others, the rhetorical perspective will generate new construals of familiar texts. Throughout we invite you to re-vision the Hebrew Scripture with us, through the lens of the rhetorical perspective.

Chapter 2

THE RHETORICAL CHARACTER
OF BIBLICAL NARRATIVE

In our introduction, we elaborated a rhetorical approach to interpreting the Bible which we suggested was consonant with its nature as Scripture, as well as being a logical extension of form criticism. Our use of the term rhetoric there referred to the means by which a text establishes its relationship to its audience in order to achieve a particular effect. In this general sense of the term, which classical scholar George Kennedy calls 'secondary rhetoric',[1] any text may be said to be rhetorical insofar as it uses language to achieve an effect upon an audience. Rhetoric of this sort is 'secondary', because it uses the stylistic resources of language not directly in the service of persuading an audience, but derivatively to affect the audience in any of a variety of ways: to inspire, to enlighten, etc.

Discourse which uses these resources directly to persuade may be characterized as 'primary rhetoric': employing language in the 'art of persuasion', as first conceptualized by the Greeks. In the present chapter, we argue that the Bible's main form of exposition, the narrative, is most appropriately characterized as primary rhetoric, its primary objective being to persuade its audience.

Surprisingly, as Professor Kennedy observes in his survey, although there are various signs of persuasive intent throughout the text, 'there is no established tradition of approaching the Old Testament as primary rhetoric'.[2] Before embarking on our argument, we should note some of the reasons for this studied resistance on the part of both ancient and modern commentators to making any association between Scripture and rhetoric as the art of persuasion.

Ancient Biblical commentators like like Origen and St. Augustine, who were familiar with classical rhetoric, appear to have perceived a contradiction between the Bible as the word of God and the Bible as

rhetoric. As Origen puts the matter, 'If our books had attracted men to belief because they were composed with rhetorical skill or with philosophical cleverness, our faith would undoubtedly have been supposed to rest in the skillful use of words and in human wisdom, and not in the power of God'. He concludes that there is 'no taint of human eloquence. . . mingled with the truth of the doctrines'.[3]

Augustine's view is a bit more complicated. While he suggests (somewhat defensively) that the Bible is 'eloquent' in a way suited to its authors' purposes, it is a strange sort of eloquence indeed. Its main characteristic seems to be its obscurity, which Augustine suggests the authors used

> for the purpose of exercising and sharpening, as it were, the minds of the readers and of destroying fastidiousness and stimulating the desire to learn, concealing their intention in such a way that the minds of the impious are either converted to piety or excluded from the mysteries of the faith.[4]

Its artful obscurity leads Augustine to treat the text primarily as poetic rather than rhetoric, and more specifically to analyze it as allegory in order to uncover the text's hidden meaning. In his discussion of rhetoric *per se* in Book IV of *On Christian Doctrine*, he strongly recommends against imitating the obscuring 'eloquence' of Scripture and has nothing specific to say about the Bible as rhetoric, beyond defending the appropriateness of its obscurity.

In contemporary Biblical studies as well, we find the term rhetoric at the periphery of textual analysis at best, but not applied directly to a characterization of the text itself. A prime example is the very active school of rhetorical critics in Biblical scholarship. These critics have limited themselves to a careful examination of the Bible's tropes and figures or, further down the line, to a delineation of the different literary genres in the text—all exercises in secondary rhetorical analysis;[5] but there is no systematic engagement of the text as primary rhetoric or persuasive discourse. While the reluctance of classical commentators to examine the Bible as rhetorical discourse might have been due to theological concerns, the reluctance of contemporary scholars is more mundanely academic. There is simply no manifestly rhetorical culture from which the Hebrews could have borrowed the idea of artfully casting their religious texts as persuasive discourse until after the majority of the texts were composed and edited. Scholars of Rabbinic literature comfortably find all manner of explicitly rhetorical forms in the Midrash and

Talmud because their appearance in Rabbinic texts can be explained by the Rabbis' familiarity with certain aspects of Greek culture.[6] But scholars have an understandable reluctance even to look for something that would not be explainable as having come from somewhere else, and the authors of the vast majority of the Biblical narratives had no access to the Greek concept of rhetoric as the art of persuasion.

But is such borrowing a necessary prerequisite for the appearance of primary rhetorical discourse? We agree with Kennedy that it is not.[7] The Greeks merely became intellectually conscious of an impulse which is part of our repertoire as symbol users. As the Greeks applied that impulse to the art of political discourse, the Hebrews applied it to narrative, but they did not conceptualize it, for such conceptualizing was foreign to the modes of discourse in which they were engaged.

But where does one look to support the identification of a genre which is not a borrowing from an already known usage, but is rather a striking innovation? The obvious danger here is imposing a frame on the discourse which is foreign and alien to its nature—which will skew one's interpretation in a direction quite divergent from the author's original intent. The way to avoid this sort of subjectivist overlay upon the text is to find support for such a reading in the text itself and in its very early interpretive history.

When one looks to the Old Testament for suggestions as to what sort of interpretation would be most faithful to the text, one finds a number of different textual cues which seem to lend support to the argument for the rhetorical approach to interpreting the text. Specifically, the cues we will examine in this regard are, first, that the narrators themselves construed God's actions in the world, the subject of their narratives, as rhetorical. The point here is that it is appropriate for subsequent interpreters to bear a relationship to the Biblical narratives similar to the one the authors of those narratives bore to their subject matter. If the authors construed God's actions as having an essentially rhetorical signification, that would suggest very strongly that they intended their own work to be so interpreted.

Second, a probable explanation for the authors' choice of the prose narrative form is that it lends itself to rhetorical purposes. Thus their own choice of form can be seen as an imitation of the divine rhetorical impulse about which they were writing, so adding a second link to the rhetorical chain.

Third, direct prescriptions in the text itself about its ritual use strongly suggest a rhetorical perspective, a suggestion supported by certain stylistic choices made by the authors.

And finally, from the very start, the Rabbinic interpreters of the Old Testament appear to have followed these prescriptions in their interpretation, which frames the text as something very much like what we would call rhetoric. Thus we will find a common thread running through the development of Biblical narrative, from the relationship of the authors to their own subject matter, through their choices of form and style, and culminating in the relationship of the earliest interpreters to the text—a thread which can clearly be identified as rhetorical and which suggests very strongly that the text can most faithfully be engaged as primary rhetoric.

The Biblical Authors' Conception of Divine Activity

Any characterization of Biblical narrative which is to be at all faithful to the intent of the authors must begin with their conception of God's activity in the world. It is clear that they thought they were communicating the word of God and as such their own words must somehow imitate his. Whatever they thought he was doing through his worldly interventions contained in the oral and written traditions on which their work was based must be their purpose as well in the narratives they composed for future generations. Thus, if we can establish that the Biblical authors conceived of God's words and actions as having an essentially rhetorical function, then we might assume it is likely that they intended their own words to function in a similar manner.

It should be noted that it is quite beyond the conventional presumptions of interpreters to try to imagine how an author might 'invent' a divine protagonist, but we have tried to manage this presumption sensibly by keeping it in close proximity to the contours of the textual object. Additional evidence in support of these imaginings is garnered from those cognate texts which were very likely a part of the authors' inventional resources.

Our argument that the Biblical authors construed God's motive for acting in the world as rhetorical begins with their studied avoidance, in the creation narratives in Genesis, of any theobiography that would give rise to what we might call a dramatistic motive for divine action. We know nothing of God's life that would explain his actions as a natural outgrowth of his character. This avoidance is

significant because the correlate mythological material from which the Biblical authors borrowed so much, grounds divine activity, especially the gods' creation of the world, precisely in such dramatistically framed motives.[8] The dramatic conflicts that grow out of the gods' character flaws and their life with one another lead them to create the world in which humans live. The gods and human beings all live amidst the same interplay of forces and share the emotional yearnings which motivate dramatic action. Greed, lust, desire for power, all serve to move the actions of the characters in the mythic dramas forward. Because action is grounded in the turmoil of conflict rather than an all-knowing will, the actions of the gods themselves contain no moral message as to how human beings should live. The gods' behavior is motivated by the behavior of other gods and in turn affects human beings fortuitously as innocent bystanders.[9]

In place of such expected dramatistic motives, the Biblical authors substitute a moralizing impulse for divine action which by contrast clearly emerges as rhetorical. We see this rhetorical motive emerging clearly in the creation narratives. In the Priestly account, there are no other divine beings in the scene of creation to conflict with God and thereby provide motivation for his action. The lifeless void that precedes creation has been purified of all possible sources of dramatic motive. But the very absence of the sources for a dramatic motive prepares the way for a rhetorical motive for his interventions in the world. With God alone and all powerful in the scene of creation, there are no other actors or sources of resistance in the story to limit God's realization of his vision. He need only speak and the world comes into existence precisely according to his will. He even responds to his own creative acts and pronounces each one good and at the end renders his judgment of the whole as very good or 'perfect'.[10] Thus the creation of the world is completed perfectly according to plan by God alone in the creation story which begins the canon.

It is left for the Yahwist narrative in ch.2 of Genesis to introduce the only source of imperfection in God's created world: the acts of human beings. In ch.1, 'P' completed his story of creation with human beings confined to being mere objects in God's perfectly orchestrated creation. Human beings never act in ch.1, but are only acted upon. In chs 2 and 3, they begin to act on their own volition, wreaking havoc with God's vision of perfection elaborated in ch.1, thus laying the groundwork for all of God's future interventions in

the world, and, not incidentally, for more story. The removal of the imperfections introduced by human action from the very start constitute the primary reason for God's involvement in the world subsequent to creation, and the basis of the story line in the rest of the Bible. The Priestly creation narrative in ch.1 and the Yahwist 'Paradise' narrative in ch.2 juxtapose the perfection of God's creation with the imperfection introduced by human action to suggest God's motive for acting: to guide human behavior in accordance with his will, thereby enabling the restoration of his original perfect vision. In response to human actions, God adjusts his view of the place of human beings in the world in 3.17ff. This re-envisioning is the 'point' of the Paradise narrative: God's activity in the world is conceptualized as a response to human action—a response which defines the new part human life shall play in the divine plan, its moral place in the universe.

This characterization of God's action in the world as 'rhetorical' is based on Lloyd Bitzer's elegantly naturalistic conceptualization of what constitutes rhetorical activity: namely, a response to a particular sort of situation which he terms rhetorical. A rhetorical situation is one in which there exists 'an imperfection. . . a defect. . . something waiting to be done. . . a thing which is other than what it should be'.[11] The rhetor's response attempts to correct the situation *through* the audience—to get the audience to make it right by affecting them through discourse. By their actions in God's created world, human beings create a situation which we can identify as rhetorical in the sense just described. The Bible's narrative discourse unfolds as the story of those exigencies and God's attempts to 'correct' them through his interventions. His actions thus have a 'rhetorical' meaning. They guide the audience in living their lives in accordance with God's perfect vision of how things should be. Understood in this way, God's worldly interventions recorded in the Biblical narratives serve as a guide to making the realization of his vision a continual possibility in history.

A more direct statement of the authors' rhetorical view of divine activity is contained in the Exodus narratives which can be said to be at the core of Jewish Biblical theology. In the Hebrew Bible, God's will is revealed in his law. The central argument advanced by the text for obedience to that law is that God delivered Israel from slavery in Egypt, thereby making them his people.[12] They are therefore obligated to obey his law. The rhetorical support for this elegantly simple formulation of Israel's obligation is the burden of most of the

pentateuchal narratives describing God's activity.

God is portrayed as first predicting the course of history and then making it happen as he predicted before the eyes of his audience. Thus the text frames the whole patriarchal history and descent into Egypt and slavery as a fulfillment of God's promise to Abraham (Gen. 15.13-14). God manipulates history as a rhetor manipulates any medium to prove his point to his audience. His point in this case is abundantly clear: As the God of history, he controls what happens and therefore he is solely responsible for Israel's deliverance from Egypt.

The individual acts comprising the Exodus itself are literally 'staged' to highlight God's power and so to prove beyond all doubt that only he could have performed this great feat. Exod. 10.1-2 provides a typical example:

> Then the Lord said to Moses 'Go to pharaoh. For I have hardened his heart and the hearts of his courtiers in order that I may display these My signs among them and that you may recount in the hearing of your sons and of your sons' sons how I made a mockery of the Egyptians and how I displayed My signs among them—in order that you may know that I am the Lord'.

God hardens Pharaoh's heart to create a situation in which he can 'show his signs' most convincingly to his audience. In Deut. 4.32-35, the primary events of the Exodus are catalogued and their rhetorical function made explicit:

> You have but to inquire about bygone ages that came before you, ever since God created man on earth, from one end of heaven to the other: has anything as grand as this ever happened, or has its like ever been known? Has any people heard the voice of a god speaking out of a fire, as you have, and survived? Or has any god ventured to go and take for himself one nation from the midst of another by prodigious acts, by signs and portents, by war, by a mighty and outstretched arm and awesome power, as the Lord your God did for you in Egypt before your very eyes? It has been clearly demonstrated to you that the Lord alone is God; there is none beside him.

God's deliverance of Israel from Egypt was singular and unique and in response Israel's commitment to his law must be complete and all consuming: 'He is your God, who wrought for you all those marvelous, awesome deeds that you saw with your own eyes. . . Love therefore the Lord your God, and always keep his charge, his laws his

rules, and his commandments' (Deut. 10.21-11.1). This transaction, as narratively conceived in Exodus and Deuteronomy, rhetorically constitutes the Jewish People. By responding to this charge, based on the 'argument' of the Exodus narratives, the Jews literally become who they are. The constitution of his 'covenant community' as he means it to be thus represents the essence of the rhetorical significance of God's activity in the world.

The Choice of the Narrative Form

We now wish to suggest that the choice of the narrative form itself represents an imitation of this same rhetorical impulse to bring the world in closer accord with God's will. The evidence indicates that Biblical narrative was an innovative form of prose art not seen before in the ancient Near East.[13] The Biblical authors appear to have developed this new form because they found the already existing literary forms available to them, namely the chronicle and the epic, so inadequate to their purposes. We can learn more about the significance of this innovation by examining the narrative as over against these other options.

Hayden White has nicely distinguished between the chronicle and the narrative as two possible forms that historical writing might take.[14] The former, represented in the ancient Near East by the king lists, gives the author little or no opportunity for moralizing—for putting events into a context indicating their significance. Narrative, on the other hand, necessitates the adding of moral significance to events in the very act of telling a story about them. White convincingly shows that a story cannot be told without inventing connections between events—connections which lend moral direction to the story as a whole. Narrative sequence cannot exist without a moral universe to make the sequence meaningful. Thus when history is adapted to the narrative form, it acquires a rhetorical thrust as events are given moral import.

The part that the imaginative embellishments of narrative play in this rhetorical thrust is nicely articulated by White:

> We can comprehend the appeal of historical (narrative) discourse by recognizing the extent to which it makes the real desirable, makes the real into an object of desire, and does so by its imposition, upon events that are represented as real, of the formal coherency that stories possess.[15]

The Biblical narratives are written as history which makes them 'real', but the fictional embellishments make the real into an object of desire. The peculiar blend of history and fiction which make up the Biblical narratives has always been difficult for scholars to explain. But when we understand this blend as the product of a choice by the narrators to write down their material as history to give it an appropriately real cast, but using the resources of narrative fiction to give it rhetorical force, the rationale for the blend becomes clear. The narrative form as they employed it was much better suited than the chronicle as a way to realize the divine rhetorical impulse: By placing God's historical interventions in a coherent narrative frame, the meaning of those interventions for how people should live their lives could be made persuasive—made into 'an object of desire'.

This realization of God's purpose through the narrativizing of sacred history emerges still more clearly when we see the choice to employ narrative as also a rejection of the epic. Where the king list and report were used for the writing of much 'history' in the ancient Near East, the epic was used to embody the theology of the great religions. The Biblical writers appear to have been sensitive to the fact that the Mesopotamian polytheism with which their own theology made a decisive break was intimately bound up with the epic form as the ideal medium for its expression. The epic lent itself nicely to ritual reenactments of the cosmic dramas which were central to Mesopotamian religion. The events as described in the epics had the magical power to repeat themselves here on earth if properly reenacted as ritual. The best example is the Akkadian Akitu ceremony wherein *Enuma Elish*, the story of creation, was acted out with ritual precision every new year. This reenactment literally had the power to begin the world anew. In their iconic plasticity, the epics metaphorically parallel the relationship between the Mesopotamians and their gods. The gods were powerful to be sure, but as cosmic objects whose power could be appropriated through correctly employed ritual procedures. The epics were 'objects' to be similarly used.

Many of the stories, such as the creation and flood accounts, contained in these epics are repeated in the Old Testament, but the form changes from the epic to the prose narrative. Although, of course, some of the content changes in the transposition as well, what is significant for us here and rarely noted is the change in form. By this change, the Biblical narrators suggest that there was something 'wrong' in the way the epics told the story, perhaps

because of the way the epic could be ritually used to relate to the deity. Thus, when the Biblical authors retold these old stories in a new way, they were not only implicitly saying that their version was the 'true story', but perhaps more importantly, that their version was the correct way to tell it, meaning that the story was to function in a new way as part of a new relationship to God.

It might appear that we are stretching the significance of a change in form, but it must be remembered that in a world where formula meant sanctity, a departure from formula made a powerful statement. In the absence of philosophy or abstract argument, one important way to move a community from one way of relating to divinity to another would be to change the form of the sacred text, the medium through which the community related to the deity.

In contrast to the epic form, the Biblical narratives do not present events with the iconic clarity that enables ritual imitation. Rather the events are presented with a kind of objectivity that leaves the narratives spare in detail and emotional color. The events are left to 'tell themselves' with only the embellishments needed to make the real desirable, persuasive. The power of the narratives is in their appeal as a 'true and objective' telling of the history of humankind, not in their magical efficacy. Thus the 'ethos' of the narratives is a metaphor for the authority of the god they tell about. The authority of both exists as a rhetorical transaction with human judgment. To affect that judgment in such a way as to engender a 'correct decision' is the objective of both this god's activity in the world and the narratives employed to describe that activity.

The Narratives Prescribe for their Correct Interpretation

The narratives themselves also make clear that this God cannot be 'used' as were the gods of other Mesopotamian religions, and that his story is to have a rhetorical rather than a magical function. Where the Mesopotamians put amulets and icons to ward off evil, the Israelites are commanded to symbolically place the story of the Exodus.[16] And where the central epics of Mesopotamian polytheism were employed in magical ceremonies, the Hebrews are commanded to tell the story of the Exodus in a rhetorical celebration which has become the Passover *Seder*.

The *Seder* as a compendium of rhetorical re-tellings of the Exodus story is based on a verse in Deuteronomy which reads,

> When, in time to come, your children ask you, 'What mean the
> decrees, laws, and rules that the Lord our God has enjoined upon you?'
> you shall say to your children, 'We we slaves to Pharaoh in Egypt
> and the Lord freed us from Egypt with a mighty hand' (6.20-21).

Thus Israel is commanded to retell this story again and again in
order to induce each succeeding generation to obey God's law. In this
verse and others like it, the text appears to prescribe how it is to be
interpreted: It is to become the heuristic basis for more stories which
are to continue God's work of inducing his people to obey his law.

The text is also written in a way that permits, even encourages it to
be interpreted in this way. Eric Auerbach in his famous comparison
between the Bible and Homer speaks of the former as being 'fraught
with background'. Whereas Homer 'represents phenomena in a fully
externalized form', leaving little or nothing to the imagination, the
Bible is full of lacunae. Thus the Biblical narratives through the
spare reticence of their style can insinuate themselves into the reality
of future generations through rhetorical interpretation. Homer, in
contrast, 'can be analyzed ... but he cannot be interpreted', as
Auerbach puts it.[17] Would it be going too far to suggest that by
leaving these eminently interpretable gaps and ambiguities in the
text, the authors and editors were indeed providing for the
continuing influence of the text through interpretation? This
possibility is supported by the often repeated direction the text gives
for its own use:

> Take to heart these instructions with which I charge you this day.
> Impress them upon your children. Recite them when you stay at
> home and when you are away, when you lie down and when you
> get up (Deut. 6.6-7).

Yet the words upon which they are to dwell in their teaching and
speaking are full of obscurities, contradictions, gaps and ambiguities.
It would seem, then, that interpretation is a necessary consequence
of this mandated concentration upon the text. Furthermore, the sort
of interpretation called for must be spoken with a rhetorical cast.
After all, if the Bible's words are indeed to be taken seriously, they
must be continually understood in application to changing circumstances. Such applications are made possible by the ambiguous
spaces left open in the text's meaning. Those spaces could be filled by
rhetorical reenactments for future generations of the text's meaning.
Thus, within the context of the command to meditate upon upon the
text, its shape and contours, what it says and what it doesn't say,

seem to suggest that it be interpreted rhetorically: that the teaching and speaking on the text be framed as persuasive appeals to future generations to live according to God's word. As we shall see, the Rabbis followed this suggestion with a vengeance.

Rabbinic Interpretation

From the very start, stories were added to fill in the gaps and shed light upon the obscurities. These stories could adapt the message to the needs and exigencies of future generations under the guise of interpreting obscure verses. Thus could the authority of the sacred text be applied to creating new messages for new situations without essentially tampering with the original—a very effective rhetorical technique requiring the cooperation of the text in order to succeed. Based on the gaps and obscurities, the Rabbis assured themselves and their audiences that they had this cooperation—that the Biblical text never stood by itself but was always in need of interpretation. Because this need for interpretation seemed a deliberate part of the text's structure, the Rabbis could claim that the interpretative tradition began with revelation at Mount Sinai simultaneously with the Biblical text itself.[18] This would seem to be a Rabbinic parallel of the contemporary hermeneutical notion that interpretation is not rooted either in the interpreter's present nor in the fixed past of the text, but rather within a fluid tradition of interpretation which connects the interpreter and the text by fusing the horizons between the two.[19]

For the most part, scholars see Rabbinic interpretation more in dialogue with its Hellenistic present than its Biblical past.[20] It is a naturally more appealing scholarly exercise to find parallels between elements of Greco-Roman culture and Rabbinic interpretation. These parallels are facilitated by the well-known Hellenistic influences geographically present during the development of the Midrash and Talmud. It is more difficult to establish the connection between Rabbinic interpretation and the Biblical text itself. The Rabbis' fanciful claim that the essence of their interpretations was revealed at Sinai along with the actual text and had more or less equal status has an obviously self-serving strategic import, and therefore does not add any weight to the case for a legitimate hermeneutical connection between Rabbinic interpretation and the Bible. There are also many significant differences between the two to support those who hypothesize a discontinuity.[21]

For our purposes, however, there is one striking similarity between Rabbinic interpretation and the Bible as well as a dissimilarity between Rabbinic and Greek thought which must be noted. Like the Bible, a central form in Rabbinic interpretation is the narrative. On the other hand, there is a total absence of anything like Greek philosophy in Rabbinic thought even though the possibilities for borrowing philosophical motifs were there. This preference for narrative as over against another prevalent motif is reminiscent of an earlier preference for narrative over the dominant epic form. The Rabbis' preference for the narrative form can also be seen as a corollary of the Bible's innovative narrative theology.

The Bible begins with one very clear and unambiguous assertion which appears to determine that the primary mode of Biblical interpretation will be narrative rather than philosophy. That assertion is that the creation of the world is an unexplainable willing, a seemingly arbitrary exercise of authority. Why does God create the world? We are not told. Philosophy, especially as practiced by the Greeks, requires that there be certain axioms—first principles— which provide a solid grounding for reality. But the Biblical doctrine of creation presents no such solidly grounded first principles. 'In the beginning, God created heaven and earth. . . ' All is contingent upon the seemingly arbitrary exercise of God's will, implying very strongly that it all could have been otherwise. This contingent quality is the stuff of stories and of rhetoric, not of philosophy.

The story particularizes one possibility among the many that could have been. The choice to tell it this way rather than that is one of strong moral import. The narrator strongly implies that it happened this way rather than that for a reason, a reason that has to do with the moral order of the world as the narrator sees it. Further understanding of the narrator's insight is discovered not by philoso- phizing but by further storytelling. Philosophy looks to the universal to explain the particular. The story pursues a particular, seemingly arbitrary possibility for the universal meaning it might hold.

This pursuit of meaning in the world of contingent possibilities through narrative rather then philosophy is reminiscent of Aristotle's placement of rhetoric as over and against science. Interpretation through narrative as the Rabbis practiced it is not idle storytelling, but rather a philosophy-like exercise of truth-seeking in the realm of the contingent. The truth lay in a very indeterminate form, contained in God's responses to human action as described in the Bible. Such truth is forever contingent upon the arbitrary comings

and goings of human behavior. Thus the form of discourse in which these truths are embodied must be continually adaptable, rather than rigidly didactic.

The narrative form carries an indeterminacy of meaning which is ideally suited to the unpredictable, changing course of human events. The truths revealed by God through his actions remains a continuing source of rhetorical topics for further application through narrative. And, of course, the Rabbinic narratives carry with them the same indeterminacy of meaning as did the original Biblical stories and so continue to be a heuristic basis for more narrative homilies responding to later rhetorical exigencies.

We might note, in passing, that the Rabbis' interpretation of the Bible through the narrative form suggests an interesting solution to a problem in the theory of interpretation. Contemporary hermeneutics, especially as formulated by Gadamer, emphasizes the historical situation of the interpreter as the all-important determinant of a text's meaning. The dialectic between the text and the exigencies of the interpreter's historicity produces the continual working out of the possibilities of the text's meaning. As Gadamer puts it, understanding always takes place in application.[22] But the weight of the interpreter's historicity leaves the text with too little power in the dialectic. E.D. Hirsch notes this problem in Gadamer's hermeneutics where satisfying the exigencies of applying the text becomes the main criterion for the validity of an interpretation, making it possible for any interpretation to be as valid as it is rhetorically effective.[23]

But the Rabbis balance the weight of the rhetorical exigencies calling for a particular application of the text by formulating their interpretation in the language of the text itself, i.e., as narrative. In this way, they are able to check their interpretation against the original, for it must not only speak effectively to their own audience, but must be faithful to the text as well: It must fit convincingly into the gaps and lacunae left by the indeterminacy of the original. It does not do to complete the story in a way that satisfies rhetorically while grating against the original story. The story must represent another plausible narrative possibility: 'It could have been this way . . . '

By keeping their interpretation to the narrative form, the Rabbis continued the search for the right way to tell the story for their particular time and place. Their faith is that God's will would continue to emerge in the world through truth seeking retellings of the story.

Narrative was ideally suited to this task, for it seems to possess a recalcitrance against becoming 'mere rhetoric'—a technique for saying anything one wishes. Interpreters of sacred texts find themselves with a dual responsibility, not uncommon to rhetors in general, of having to induce their audience to right action through the application of a sacred text to a new situation while at the same time remaining faithful to the truth of the 'original'. The narrative form is suited to fulfilling both responsibilities, when the source of 'topics', the rhetor's text, is likewise cast in the narrative form; for then the interpretive story can be assessed for its fidelity to the narrative idea of the original. Thus, Rabbinic midrash suggests that the rhetorical power of a narrative text to speak to an audience can be most faithfully transmitted through a narrative interpretation of that text.

Alisdair MacIntyre characterizes this power which inheres in narrative as follows: '. . . to ask who we are, is to ask of what story are we a part'.[24] MacIntyre suggests that one of the difficulties in agreeing upon the virtues and teaching them in contemporary times is that we no longer have a communal story in which to ground them.[25] The Biblical authors as well as the Rabbinic interpreters of the Bible who employed the narrative form brought the authority of the Bible's narrative tradition to bear on their own prescriptions for right living by continually finding the source for those prescriptions in the story of which they and their people were a part. Or as the Rabbis themselves put it: 'Wouldst thou come to know Him who spoke and the world came to be. Then study Aggadah [narrative midrash] for by that means thou dost come to know the Holy One Blessed be He and to cleave to His ways'.[26]

Conclusion

Thus concludes our examination of the suggestions found in the Biblical text as well as in Rabbinic interpretation that the text is most appropriately interpreted as primary rhetoric. The analysis yielded a consistent view of the text as rhetoric, reflected in the author's view of the subject matter, in direct indications in the text itself prescribing its 'usage', in the author's choice of the narrative form, and in the Rabbis' midrashic interpretation. If we may depend on the text itself as an authoritative guide to its appropriate interpretation, then it is clear that the Old Testament narratives may properly be

interpreted as rhetorical discourse. This does not obviate the importance of all the 'rhetorical studies' of the Bible's literary art, but merely bids us to use the insights from those studies to understand better how the narratives function as persuasive discourse. Such an approach would seem to follow Matthew Arnold's eloquently stated view of the task of Biblical interpretation:

> But matters are not at all mended by taking their language [the language of the Biblical authors] of approximate figure and using it for the language of scientific definition; or by crediting them with our own dubious science, deduced from metaphysical ideas which they never had. A better way than this, surely, is to take their fact of experience, to keep it steadily for our basis in using their language to see whether using their language with the ground of this real and firm sense to it, as they themselves did, somewhat of their feeling may not grow upon us.[27]

Chapter 3

A RHETORICAL VIEW OF HISTORICAL NARRATIVE

When we come to the more ostensibly historical narratives of
Exodus, the 'best text' approach runs into some serious snags.
Because the narratives purport to be history, scholars have worked to
assess the faithfulness of their correspondence to known historical
'facts'. One of the main resources relating to their credibility as
history, of course, is the actual date of the documents; and so
extensive investigations have focused on whether the narratives were
actually written at a time when they could have accurately reported
the events they describe.

While these pursuits have yielded some interesting hypotheses and
supporting data, they have proved something of a distraction from
the search for the best text. Not surprisingly, scholars have found
that these texts liberally sprinkled their alleged reporting of events
with fictive elements reflecting later political and religious concerns.
So considered as histories, in the modern sense of factual reportage,
the status of these texts as the best texts they can be is considerably
undermined. As Hans Frei has observed,

> In effect, the realistic or history-like quality of biblical narrative,
> acknowledged by all, instead of being examined for the bearing it
> had in its own right on meaning and interpretation was decidedly
> transposed into the quite different issue of whether or not the
> narrative was historical.[1]

But it seems that Frei equivocates here as well. By reading the texts
as 'history-like', he tries to give the texts their generic due as the
histories they purport to be, while at the same time taking account of
their obvious propensity for fictionalizing. But this also falls short of
a best text reading, for these texts have remained profoundly

persuasive for over 2000 years despite the fact that their inconsistencies and inaccuracies have been apparent almost from the very beginning. They have been persuasive because their truth-claims have been found credible. The rhetorical critic, seeking after a best text reading, must therefore ask, 'In what sense can these texts be taken as true?'

Frei assumes that if they are not factually true, the only alternative is to read them as realistic fiction. Hayden White's well-known argument that historical narrative requires fictive inventions to fill out the narrative frame, distorting the actual sequence of events by delimiting beginnings and endings, lends further credence to Frei's reading by suggesting that there is no real difference between history and realistic fiction.[2] The fact that they are both shaped by essentially the same exigencies of narrativizing means that they can be interpreted in the same way.

Our present task of finding a best text reading of the Bible's historical narratives requires that we first ascertain whether indeed there is a significant difference between reading these texts as history or as realistic fiction. This chapter argues that it indeed does make a difference to our understanding, at least in the case of the Biblical narratives, to read a text as history rather than realistic fiction. We will then look at the narratives themselves for indications of whether they mean to be read as one or the other, and if it is more appropriate to read them as history, history of what sort.

The generic question is especially important here because of the 'rhetorical fact' that these narratives have 'rung true' to at least one important segment of their intended audience: They have been taken by the Jewish community as their true history—and not because they are necessarily factual, nor because they merely express some artistically framed 'truth about life'. We will find that close attention to the rhetorical shape of these narratives suggests another possible way of understanding the truth claims of purportedly historical discourse.

Fiction and History

As exemplars of the Bible's historical narratives, we have chosen two passages in Deuteronomy (6.20-25; 26.5-10) which summarize the events described in the pentateuchal histories. We chose them because they reflect the basic shape of the pentateuchal material in skeletal form and so might reveal formal aspects of the histories not

readily apparent in their more intricate complex versions.[3]

The summary which appears in Deut. 26.5-10 reads as follows:

> My father was a fugitive Aramean. He went down to Egypt with meager numbers and sojourned there; but there he became a great and populous nation. The Egyptians dealt harshly with us and oppressed us; they imposed heavy labor upon us. We cried to the Lord, the God of our Fathers, and the Lord heard our plea and saw our plight, our misery, and our oppression. The Lord freed us from Egypt by a mighty hand, by an outstretched arm and awesome power, and by signs and portents. He brought us to this place and gave us this land, a land flowing with milk and honey. Wherefore I now bring the first fruits of the soil which you, O Lord, have given me.

Now the most obvious characteristic of the passage and of the pentateuchal histories generally is that they are presented in the narrative form. Because narrative is the medium for both history and fiction, the narrativity of the passage alone is not conclusive. Indeed it is this very ambiguity of narrative and its strong suggestion of fictive invention that has made it possible for interpreters of the text to speak of historicized fiction, fictionalized history, and allegory, while still claiming to be faithful to the text.

However, we can specify the type of narrative it is a bit further, by noting that it is realistic, i.e., that it portrays events which could have happened in the world as the reader knows it; and also that it is didactic—it has a point to make. These characteristics of the narrative before us still leave both possibilities open: It could be read as history or as realistic fiction. We are now ready to examine the differences between reading this text as realistic didactic narrative and as history in a didactic cast to see if the text itself gives us grounds for choosing one way of reading it over the other.

The didactic narrative is coterminous with Aristotle's *exemplum*, which along with the *enthymeme* can be seen as a central method of using language to move people to action. Narratives which are more realistic accomplish the aims of the *exemplum* differently from those which are less realistic.

At the less realistic end of the continuum we have the fable. The fable makes its claims very softly upon the audience, for as Susan Suleiman observes, it assumes the cooperation of the audience, i.e., that 'rebellious readers, or merely indifferent ones do not exist'.[4] So rather than pushing or coercing the audience into a moral commitment based on its message, the fable leaves the audience to draw the moral

implications from the story as it will. The fable obviously has a point to make, but because the created, fantastic world of the fable is not the real world of the audience, there is no necessary reason that one should affect the other. One has time to enjoy the fable and reflect on its message. There is no sense of persuasive urgency in the telling. Of course, the teller of the fable can wield other sorts of coercive power over the auditors and thereby make more compelling claims on their behavior, but that is not a function of the form itself.

The more realistic didactic story exercises somewhat greater endogenous power over the reader. Here readers are offered a model of life that could be theirs. The power of a vision of life as it should be, artfully portrayed, is seen by many to be greater in its capacity to move people than actual history. But insofar as the narrative is not grounded in claimed historicity, the reader still has the capacity to abrogate its power, to rescind his or her willing suspension of disbelief.

This rescission, not even always under the reader's control, is what constantly threatens the didactic hold that fiction might have over its readers. At any moment, a wedge might be driven between the reader and a world that could become real for him or her. The reader must also expend energy helping the author maintain the illusion of reality—energy which diverts the reader from becoming fully immersed in the story. Because the point of a narrative, the truth it has to tell, is embedded in the story rather than detachable from it, we can see that insofar as a story is merely realistic, its capacity to address the auditor directly and forcefully from within itself is limited. As with the fable, readers have considerable leeway in the capacity they grant the narrative to address them directly and authoritatively.

On the other hand, a narrative which makes a claim to historicity takes a much more aggressive and direct stand in relationship to the audience. The events portrayed in a historical narrative happened in the real world and so have a forward movement that carries directly into the world of the reader. He or she exists in the same world as the events portrayed and so is part of the same unfolding story the author is telling. Thus the author is able to address the reader not in the hypothetical mood: 'Consider what would happen if this story were true'; but rather confronts the reader directly with a reality in which he or she is a participant, willing or not.

There are some other significant differences between historical and fictional narrative in the way they address their respective

audiences. First, there is the nature and composition of the audience the text constructs for itself. Every discourse has an implicit construction of the audience it is addressing. The nature of the construction provides the grounds for the actual audience's relationship to the discourse. In the case of fictional narrative, the author addresses the audience as one human being to another. Even though the auditors might aggregate themselves into a group for purposes of listening to the story, the story still addresses them as individual persons. There is a certain flexibility of response implied in this mode of address. As individual persons, auditors need not feel compelled to respond as members of a community. Such membership would constrain the response because it implies that the response is both made in concert with others and in turn has its effect on the group as a whole.

So it is with history. History does not tell the story of individuals, but of a group. As such, individuals can only find themselves in the story as members of a group, for so the story construes them. Thus their response is not made in the privacy of their solitude, but in the light of their public life in the community. There is the implication, especially in national histories such as those in the Bible, that the response of the auditor has great import for the community as a whole. Indeed, in the mode of address in the two Deuteronomic narratives, the community and the individual are one. The 'you' which could be construed as referring to the individual slips quickly into 'we' and 'us', making the plural nature of the 'you' explicit and unambiguous. The individual is not free to respond idiosyncratically to the narrative, but is called upon to understand and respond to the narrative as a Jew.

This leads us to distinguish between the sorts of responses historical and fictional narratives attempt to elicit from their respective audiences. As has been observed by many, perhaps most notably Kenneth Burke,[5] a narrative gets through to the auditor by moving the auditor to identify with it. In the case of fiction, this identification is not only hypothetical, as we observed earlier, it is also vicarious: This is what happened to someone who is *like* you or me. The success of the story depends in large measure on the author's capacity to get the auditor to identify with individual characters—to make that vicarious 'like' as forceful a linkage as possible. But the identification is never complete. The auditor is always living the life of the story through the characters, and usually at a safe, manageable distance.

The force of the identification is achieved through the verisimilitude of the portrayal and other somewhat less tangible aspects of the narrative's aesthetic character.[6] Insofar as the truth of the tale can be corroborated, it is essentially an aesthetic corroboration of the author's artistic vision. If it is consistently beautiful enough to attract us into its world and keep us there, and if what we find in that world comports with our reality, then the story's claim upon us has gone as far as it can go. Its corroborated truth remains aesthetic: That which is corroborated is the artful construction of the narrative itself.

This sort of corroboration of a narrative's truth value through an appreciation of its artfulness is recounted in Robert Alter's work, *The Art of Biblical Narrative*.[7] Alter has done much to open the Bible to a serious reading by a wider audience, but by limiting himself to aesthetic judgments, he still does not integrate the Bible's truth-claims, as they are spoken, into his interpretative approach. He essentially reads the text as realistic fiction. In this view, the Bible's 'truth-claims' represent, at most, aesthetic truths, to be encountered and evaluated through an appreciation of the Bible's narrative art. By paying close attention to the artistic devices, the narrator's insights about life can be discovered and their correspondence to life as we live it, examined.

With history, especially of the corporate sort found in the Bible, the claim on the audience is much more profound. Rather than 'This is something which *might have* happened to someone *like you or me*', the claim is, 'This *is* what happened to *us*'. It is our story and so has profound moral implications for how we see ourselves and how we live. As is the case with didactic fiction, or any discourse which makes some sort of truth-claim, this history also provides corroboration for its claim. With realistic didactic fiction, we saw that the corroboration is provided by the aesthetic character of the artist's construction. In a corporate history, because the claim is that this story is the auditor's own, the corroboration is found in the familiarity of the story itself. Insofar as the auditors find themselves responding with the warm glow of familiar recognition: 'Yes this is who we are', the 'truth' of the story has been corroborated.

This is not the truth of facticity corroborated by reference to what actually happened, nor is it an aesthetic truth mirrored in the artist's construction; rather it is the truth of a community's identity, felt in the deepest recesses of its consciousness. When the narrative achieves its objective, the audience recognizes itself in the portrayal. They see that believing this happened to them makes them who they

are. It is in its articulation of this felt-consciousness of who they are that the narrative is corroborated as construing their past correctly.

This view of history comports with Jan Huizinga's definition of history as 'the intellectual form in which a civilization renders an account to itself of its past'.[8] The 'intellectual form' he refers to must be able to tap the civilization's tacit knowledge[9] of who they are, for it is that tacit knowledge, profound but unthematized, which makes possible the corroboration of the truth claims of the account. In the case of the pentateuchal histories, the form in which the community will be able to recognize itself is clearly the Exodus narratives.

We are not prepared to say what the more traditional historical truth value of that account might be: It might or might not be an accurate representation of the events it describes. But more importantly, its 'rhetorical' referent, the way it constitutes the Jewish people through its telling of their story, is experienced as having the same force as facticity. Our best text reading, therefore, does not deny that these narratives might reference actual events, but merely recognizes that this dimension is ancillary to the most important truth they have to tell—the truth contained in the narratives' rhetorical power to create and define a community's identity.

To put it somewhat differently, the objective of the narrative is not primarily an accurate reporting of events, but rather the sort of narrative shaping of those events which will lead the audience to believe it is their story, and so to constitute their community based on it. Rather than the truth lying in the correspondence between the story and the events it describes, this is a 'rhetorical truth', embodied in the effect of the discourse upon the audience. It is true through how it affects action in the world—its *praxis*, one might say.

Evidence of the Rhetorical Character of Biblical History

We now turn to the other Deuteronomic summary, to see further how this sort of 'rhetorical truth' is disclosed through discourse.

> When in time to come, your son asks you, 'What mean the exhortations, laws, and rules which the Lord our God has enjoined upon you?' you shall say to your son, 'We were slaves to Pharaoh in Egypt and the Lord freed us from Egypt with a mighty hand. The Lord wrought before our eyes marvelous and destructive signs and portents in Egypt, against Pharaoh and all his household; and He freed us from there, that He might take us and give us the land that he promised on oath to our fathers. Then the Lord commanded us

to observe all these laws, to revere the Lord our God, for our lasting good and for our survival, as is the case. It will be therefore to our merit before the Lord our God to observe faithfully this whole Instruction, as He has commanded us.

The entire passage is cast as a speech from parent to child, with the parent and child playing distinct and separate roles. The story begins by using 'we' and 'us', making clear its intent to join speaker and audience, past and future, in a bond created by the events described. This bonding would seem to reflect the orientation of text to auditor in the narrative as a whole. Through the telling of the story, the text means to join the auditors together into a community constituted by the events of the story, to make the story *ours* in the most profound sense of the possessive.

According to this reading, Jews can be defined as people who stake their lives on this being their story.[10] This setting down of the 'material' identity of a community in a series of historical events is no small matter. It establishes a changeless core which holds a people together over time by making it possible for successive generations to identify themselves with one another through a stable text.

Not incidentally, this passage, mandating the 'teaching' of the Exodus and its significance to children through the ages, has been used as the basis for the Passover *Seder*. In that setting, the 'we' of the passage is given the added depth of the family around the *Seder* table. The *Seder* text itself, the *Haggadah*, is a compendium of midrashic glosses on the basic story as well as accounts of significant *Seder* celebrations throughout history. Thus the family sitting together around the table can expand the range of its communal identification by connecting itself to the historical stream of retellings of the story presaged by the Biblical passage and recorded in the *Haggadah*. As the same text is repeated year after year in the same family setting, the look and sound of the Exodus becomes even more intensely familiar—as if it were an image in a family album. It would seem that the text has successfully reinforced its objective of forging the community's identity by the prescription it makes for the continued repetition of its story.

That the goal and objective of the core Biblical narratives in the Pentateuch is as we have characterized it, is further corroborated by aspects of the text beyond the basic summaries as well. The successive accretions to the core history of the Exodus, namely the patriarchal and primeval narratives, can be seen as giving solidity

and depth to the identity forged by the events of the Exodus narrative. The added stories give the community's identity an antiquity that makes that identity part of the cosmic order of things from the very beginning. The Priestly genealogies, for example, solidly connect those first days to the narrative time of the Exodus in an unbroken line. Historical critics have also shown that the most obviously invented portions of the Exodus and Settlement narratives are precisely those anachronisms which attempt to push significant aspects of the community's historical identity further and further backward in time.[11]

This same objective of supporting the identity-constituting function of the basic Exodus narrative is also reflected in the mystery of the Biblical history's abrupt ending. Hayden White has observed that the essential moral import of a history can be seen in where it chooses to begin and end its story.[12] These choices define the moral universe bounded by the story. We have already seen the significance of the story's beginning and now we must ask, 'What sort of events come to an end with the ending of the story? Why break off the history here?' The answer, in line with our thesis, is that the sorts of events which became the canonical history, are those events which constitute the identity of Israel. It is not that Israel's history stops with the Exile, but rather that those events which have the sort of 'ontological' status usually associated with myth have been satisfactorily elaborated and a break must be made.[13]

Among other cultures in the ancient Near East, events of a similar 'ontological' order, which have the power to constitute present realities, are portrayed as having taken place in mythical time. It would seem that an important difference in Israelite civilization is that those constitutive events are seen as taking place in historical time. But that time must still be set apart as 'speaking' while the rest of time 'listens', and so we have the canonical history. It must end, so that 'profane time' can begin, and the community can commence the long struggle 'to get back home'.

Defining Characteristics of the Genre

Having identified the sort of 'truth' the Biblical histories have to tell, and further elaborated how the narrative form is used to make that truth credible and compelling, we now turn specifically to a generic characterization of these narrative histories: How might we best describe the sort of history they are? Our suggestion for a generic

characterization is based on the fact that the objective we have identified for the Biblical histories is clearly a pragmatic one. The past is not examined for itself, but rather for how it can affect the present. It might be said that all history is formulated to affect the present in a particular way. So contends Lévi-Strauss is his famous dictum that there is no such thing as a history *of*, only a history *for*.[14]

Here we speak only of the Biblical histories, and in this case, the intensity of the pragmatic motive leads us to characterize the Biblical histories as rhetorical. By this we mean that the shape of Biblical narrative, its figuration, its beginning and ending, its more obviously invented portions, indeed its very coming into existence, all follow from this objective of affecting the members of the audience in a particular way: namely to constitute themselves as a community with this story as its basis.

As rhetoric, Biblical narrative is called into being by a rhetorical exigence: a situation which needs correcting through discourse.[15] In this case, the exigence is that the community's image of itself has gone awry and the existing history is inadequate to the task of moving the community to correct its vision. A new version of the story is created as a response to the situation, a story whose purpose it is to set the community's self-image straight and thus, on the basis of a new view of the past, to move the audience to right action in the present.

Although we cannot do it here, we believe that most of the later narratives, which repeat stories told by earlier narratives, have this same rhetorical function: to correct something in the community's consciousness which has gone awry and which previous histories cannot adequately adjust. Given that the 'canonized past' was the accepted source of topics for persuading audiences in ancient Israel, these topics could be embellished and reframed in the service of keeping the community's vision of itself and its God 'true'.

The status of that 'truth' depends, of course, on one's theology and metaphysics. Thus the Bible's invention of new versions of the sacred past to induce right action in the present can be seen as being as noble (or as ignoble) as any other rhetorical *topos*, and framed by the same ultimate uncertainties.

Indeed, as we have noted, Hayden White has argued that all history in the narrative form is, in large part, an invention guided by rhetorical aims.[16] Although we believe White overstates the case, his basic argument is cogent: Narrative requires that events be given a

figuration which are at best only ambiguously present in the original events.

The question is, how does the invention affect the validity or 'truth' of the narrative as history? Everyone has had the experience of telling a story and using the resources of narrative to embellish the story and thereby to connect one's hearer more compellingly to the events: to bridge the emotional distance separating one who really understands the significance of what went on from one who has yet to understand. What emerges in such narrative embellishments, one would like to think, is a 'truer picture' of what really happened. We are suggesting the Biblical authors have the same presumption.

In order to construct such a narrative, the historian-narrator must have an *a priori* overall concept of how he or she wishes to construe the events in order to formulate a system of figuration that is consistent within itself, fits the narrative form, and makes the point he or she wishes to make. But the rhetorical art of the historian is to hide his or her hand such that the reader does not see the narrative argument as consciously imposed—does not see that the historian begins with a definite concept of how the whole ties together and what it means.

The art of creating compelling historical narrative, which effectively accomplishes this inventional task of making the narrative frame credible, consists, in part, in making use of those conventions, which at a given time and place, make history authoritative by their allusions to the prevailing metaphysic. This might explain the Bible's use of certain stock motifs and character stereotypes. The presence of these conventions assures the audience that the history is authentic. They make it possible for the audience seriously to entertain its truth-claims. The Biblical narratives achieve the status of sacred history in part by having in them those motifs and aspects of characterization that one would expect in a sacred history. The same sort of argument could be made for the use of accepted scholarly conventions to conceal the inventional hand of contemporary historians and lend their accounts credibility.

In the case of the Biblical narratives, the authors' inventional resources also include other narrative construals of the events preserved by the tradition as part of the community's historical memory. When the narrator's inventional art works well, aided and abetted by the community's narratively preserved memory, the story seems to be telling itself, the historian merely letting the events unfold as they really were. And perhaps the historian's narrative does

indeed present us with a truer picture of the events as they really were than would be the case with a more spare and purely 'factual' chronology. Again one's metaphysics must guide that judgment, however uncertainly. Ultimately, there is no sure criterion for distinguishing between true and false rhetoric.

Summary

We began by arguing that there was a significant difference between reading the Bible's narrative texts as history or as realistic fiction. We then argued that the text strongly indicated that it meant to be read as history. But the kind of history it turned out to be we found was rhetorical. As we traced the implications of the rhetorical cast of Biblical history, the line between history and fiction became blurred once more, with only the dull, uncertain light of convention to help us distinguish one from the other. We found it makes a profound difference whether we read a story as history or fiction, but in the final analysis, our choice of which story to believe, of what to call history and what to call fiction, might have to be made alone and in darkness.

Chapter 4

FORENSIC NARRATION IN BIBLICAL NARRATIVE

Not too many years ago a number of critics began to raise such
serious questions about the use of the term 'history' for Old
Testament narrative[1] that many of us stopped using it. Alternatives
were coined, such as Hans Frei's 'realistic narrative'.[2] Although this
strategy had certain advantages, we can now see that it was ill-
advised. As the previous chapter shows, the narratives of the Old
Testament, particularly those which tell the nation's story, engage
the reader in such a way that the term 'history' is unavoidable.

In the stories of the patriarchs, the exodus, the conquest, the
period of the judges and the monarchy, Israelite authors were
rendering an account of the nation's past. This account was intended
to elicit the reader's identification with the people. The reader could
confirm the narrative's truth by recognizing the community's
identity in the portrait emerging from the story. This portrait
involved the memory of the people, but also its sense of its character
and destiny.

This general classification of Biblical narratives opens up interesting
possibilities for the analysis of particular narratives. Each narrative
has its own specific rhetorical dynamics within this comprehensive
horizon. Some narratives were written to tell the community one
thing about itself, others another. In this chapter we will isolate a set
of narratives which have a similar rhetorical effect in mind. We shall
apply a category of classical rhetoric, forensic speech, to a set of
narratives designed to convict or exonerate the personae of the
accounts.

The identification of the rhetorical purpose of these particular
narratives will provide us with some purchase on the question of
their historical fidelity. The general definition of rhetorical history

does not guarantee that the stories told are isomorphic with the events that happened. We must look to the specific rhetorical purpose of a given narrative to determine whether there were reasons in the situation for getting the facts straight.

Fact or Fiction?

Since the question of whether Biblical narratives are historically accurate or not has been the subject of much debate over the two centuries of critical scholarship, it is appropriate to reflect on the question at the outset. It is our view that the identification of the rhetorical purposes of a narrative will at least sharpen our focus on the questions to be asked, and at best provide compelling answers.

From time to time one meets a skeptical scholar who doubts not only the historicity of the Biblical narrative, but the capacity of ancient peoples to distinguish facts from fancy. The concept of fact, it is suggested, was a discovery or invention of modern science and historiography. Now it may well be true that the concept of a neutral, uninterpreted, discreet fact is a modern invention. On the other hand, every human society has occasions when 'facts' are important. A king needs to know the size and deployment of an enemy army before he engages in battle, and the more accurate his information is, the better his strategy. A buyer needs to know the quality of goods he is considering to purchase, and the better his knowledge, the better his dealing.

One of the most important occasions on which the 'facts' are necessary is a judicial deliberation. A court must examine testimony and evidence to decide innocence and guilt, rights and duties. An ancient court session would probably strike us as odd, but we would immediately recognize the activity as directed to the same end as our trials. That the establishment of the truth of guilt and innocence was of utmost importance to them is shown by the admonitions in legal material to seek justice and by the threats of divine sanctions for false and unjust judgments.[3]

The question is whether history-writing—Israelite history-writing in particular—was considered a situation which required getting the facts straight. How can this question be answered? One attack is to examine its mode of presentation. Robert Alter, for example, classifies Old Testament narrative as 'historicized fiction', 'fictionalized history' and just plain 'prose fiction' because it exhibits the sort of artistic invention associated with short stories and novels.

> What a close reading of a text does suggest... is that the writer could manipulate his... material with sufficient freedom and sufficient firmness of authorial purpose to define motives, relations, and unfolding themes... with the kind of subtle cogency we associate with the conscious artistry of the narrative mode designated prose fiction.[4]

This characterization of Biblical narrative justifies the sort of close reading which Alter proposes to give it; nevertheless, we believe that his exposition of selected narratives confirms his assumption. There is a circular character to all interpretation, but there is good reason to accept an assumption which produces powerful, subtle results.[5]

Meir Sternberg does not dispute Alter's characterization of Biblical narrative as artistic, but he objects to the conclusion that the employment of artistic invention implies that the narratives are to be read as fiction. Historians, he asserts, employ the very same narrative arts as fiction writers.[6] History cannot be distinguished from fiction by its formal features, but by its purpose.[7] The purpose of Biblical narratives was to remember the national history and through memory to know YHWH the God of Israel.

Sternberg's case is cogent. History is a mode of discourse which engages its reader in a particular way. However, this still does not answer the question whether history-writing in Israel was an activity which required fidelity to the facts. If the authors expected their readers to believe their accounts, not just entertain them as possible, by what logic and justification could they invent dialogs, scenes, motives and the like? *Was there something about the rhetorical situation which not only permitted but required such invention to tell the story accurately?*

The exigencies of the rhetorical situation itself raise another kind of question. If the reader of ancient history confirmed the claim of the narrative to be true by its match with the community's understanding of itself, an historian would be tempted to manufacture and manipulate the past to satisfy the national ego, justify its power structure and institutions, etc. *Were there factors in the rhetorical situation which resisted the manipulation and falsification of the nation's story?*

This question cannot be answered in the same way for all national histories. There may be a tendency for nations, both ancient and modern, to glorify and idealize their past. This does not necessarily imply wholesale fabrication, however, for many national cultures

have a strong memory and prophetic voices in the community which remind the people of what they would like to forget. Ancient Israel may well have formed a national memory which resisted the manipulations of flattering authors, and Yahwism may have provided resources for an honest, realistic assessment of the national character.

We must ask whether there was anything in the rhetorical situation of the original narrative which required the historian to take the facts into account. Was there a national memory in the audience that resisted the manipulations of flattering authors? Did Yahwism provide resources for an honest, realistic assessment of the national character?

There is at least one line of evidence that indicates that Israelite historians were forced to take unwanted facts into account. The Biblical narrative is permeated with stories which present an unflattering and unedifying image of the people of God. Since it is improbable that the people desired this self-image, what forced them to recognize themselves in it nevertheless? *What made them able and willing to remember what they would like to forget?*

In the remainder of this chapter we will argue that a particular rhetorical classification can answer these three questions: Forensic narration requires the invention of dialog, incidents and motives to weave together the known facts of a case into a story which convicts or exonerates the parties involved. Since the purpose of such a narration is to persuade the reader to judge the actions of the parties involved, it requires an account of the facts known to the reader. The cumulative force of this type of narrative in Israelite tradition induced Israelite consciousness to own up to the 'dark side' of the nation's history and character.

Forensic Narration

In this section we will offer a definition of 'forensic narration' and show that it was a standard part of Israelite judicial proceedings. This discussion will prepare the reader to judge the application of the classification to narratives which are not judicial speeches.

'Forensic' has to do with addresses to judicial bodies; the *narratio* is the portion of such a speech which recounts the 'facts' of the case in such a way as to convince the judges that the events and acts of the parties fall under a particular legal classification. What we have in the *narratio* is a genuine factual history, yet one which communicates the facts in a configuration calculated to engender a particular

judgment regarding them. As Quintillian states, 'For the statement of facts is not made merely that the judge may comprehend the case, but rather that he may look upon it in the same light as we ourselves'.[8]

Evidence for Judicial Narration in Israelite Trials

We have traces of forensic narration in Biblical law and narrative. The legal formulation known as casuistic law, found in abundance in the Book of the Covenant (Exod. 20.22–23.19) and in lesser numbers in Deuteronomy and the Holiness Code (Lev. 17.26), enunciate the 'facts' (what happened) in the protasis and rule upon their legal consequences in the apodosis.[9] For example, in the law of the goring ox (Exod. 21.28-32), the primary fact is a person who has been killed by an ox. The wound, the presence of the ox, perhaps with blood on its horns, and probably witnesses would establish what happened. The more difficult question was the culpability of the owner. He would be classified as culpable if he knew that his ox was dangerous and did nothing to restrain him. Since no one can read a man's mind, only testimony that he had been warned could establish prior knowledge. Such testimony would take the form of forensic narration.

Narration would play a central role in a trial. In a remedial action, the process of the trial would pit the story of the plaintiff against that of the defendant, and the court would seek to decide which story to believe. One strategy might be to attempt to 'crack' a suspicious story by asserting a plausible counter-story.[10] Throughout the process the court would be piecing together a 'synthetic' story which accounted for the physical evidence and testimony. Their synthesis would be the 'true' story, the story of what really happened as far as the judges could determine it; it would also be a judicial determination, for the purpose of the judicial proceedings is to subsume actions and events under legal concepts and principles.

We have some examples of forensic narration in judicial settings. The daughters of Zelophehad appeal to Moses for their father's inheritance in a brief speech with a *narratio* and a *conformatio* (argument):

narratio   Our father died in the wilderness; he was not one of the faction, Korah's faction, which banded together against the Lord, but died for his own sin; and he has left no sons.

confirmatio   Let not our father's name be lost to his clan just
                because he had no son! Give us a holding among our
                father's kinsman. (Num. 27.3-4).

This appeal is so brief that it sounds like a condensation of a more
elaborate address. It covers the essential facts of the case, including
an exoneration of their father of any guilt which would abrogate his
right to a share in the national territory and a 'name' within his
family. The fact that he has no sons leads to the argument and
request. The reader has to fill in the law of inheritance assumed in
the argument. YHWH grants the justice of their case and modifies the
rules of inheritance accordingly. The other members of the family
might have contested the appeal, since they would be in line for
Zelophehad's share, but they do not. An objection is raised later
(Lev. 36.2-4), of a deliberative rather than judicial type, and Moses
modifies the divine ruling to assure that no tribe inherits land
belonging to another.

    The appeal of the woman of Tekoa (2 Sam. 14.4-7) is more elegant
and elaborate, though still rather brief. Her *narratio* makes no
attempt to justify the son who murdered his brother, but rather
presents the case—again having to do with inheritance—as a legal
dilemma which can be resolved only by suspending the penalty for
murder. To make her case vivid, she elaborates detail, including
imaginary dialog. Her speech ends with a short but pregnant
confirmatio.

    Neither of these is an elaborate forensic narration, but they do set
forth the facts of the case in a persuasive account. Each leads toward
the legal decision that the supplicant favors, then draws out the legal
principles they would like the judge to apply. The *narratio* of the
daughters of Zelophehad cleared the deceased of any judicial
impediment to their request, while the woman of Tekoa dramatizes
the pressure of the relatives to execute the killer (perhaps hinting at
their greed as well as desire for justice). Both, thus, have in relatively
simple, rudimentary form the kind of rhetorical moves which we will
look for in the full-blown narratives.

    Although it would have been plausible to surmise the use of
forensic narration in Israelite trials without examples of it, these
examples should make the case virtually certain. They demonstrate
that the culture was familiar with a type of discourse which accorded
significance to evidence, within a persuasive argument. The employment of artistic invention would be a natural and justifiable

component of such narration, for its objective is to place the facts in a story which supports the speaker's argument. Thoughts and deeds would be imputed to the characters involved to fill in gaps; actions that appeared suspicious would be explained; appeals to rationality and character would be used to support one's story. The court's authoritative story would have to be more careful about its inferences, but it would still fill in gaps and discrepancies in the evidence and testimony, and past knowledge of the parties, suppositions as to likely occurrences, etc., would enter into the story.

Forensic Narration in Biblical Narrative

Now we have arrived at the heart of our argument. It will be argued that forensic narration was adapted by Israelite historians to persuade readers of the innocence or guilt of prominent persons in the society for which they were writing. They composed narratives which wove together the known facts or public rumors into an account of the actions of the parties involved in such a way as to elicit the reader's judgment. These narratives then invariably conclude with YHWH's declaration of the innocence or guilt of one or more of the personae.

The application of the title 'forensic narration' to a portion of a Biblical history-work has to be regarded as an analogy. The narratives under consideration are not embedded in legal addresses, but in larger narrative complexes. Hence, they are written for a reader, not a judge. What makes the classification applicable is that our Biblical narratives resemble the *narratio* of judicial addresses in their recounting of events and actions in such a way as to persuade the reader of the guilt or innocence of the actors. As if to clinch the cogency of the analogy, the Biblical narratives conclude these accounts with a quasi-judicial transaction.

Forensic narration could be used both to prosecute and to defend the parties whose story is told. There are a number of accounts in the Former Prophets which tell a story of persons coming to power with the purpose of defending them from charges of wrongdoing. The story of David's rise to power told in 1 Samuel 16–2 Samuel 7, and the account of Jehu's revolt in 2 Kings 9–10 fit this description. In each case, the usurper's legitimacy is defended by a portrayal of his and his supporters' actions as either innocent or justified.

The threats to David's legitimacy came from actions which he took in his rise to power and incidents which worked out in his

favor.[11] He had a conflict with his king, Saul, which ended in virtual
rebellion. The narrative carefully places the blame for this break on
Saul, climaxed in two para-legal encounters in the wilderness in
which Saul admits his guilt and David calls upon YHWH to be
judge.[12] David entered into the service of the Philistines when they
were at war with Israel. The narrator seeks to clear David of any
possible charge of treason.[13] The deaths of Saul, Jonathan, Abner
and Ishbaal were very fortunate for David's cause. The narrator
shows that David was not implicated in any of them, and in fact
grieved over their deaths. He goes so far as to step outside the
narrative framework to characterize the impression David was
making—and he desires to make:

> All the troops took note of it (David's mourning for Abner) and
> approved, just as all the troops approved everything else the king
> did. That day all the troops and all Israel knew that it was not by
> the king's will that Abner son of Ner was killed (2 Sam. 3.36f.).

The account reaches its conclusion with first the people of Israel
acknowledging David's legitimacy (2 Sam. 5.1-3) and then YHWH
confirming his election of David and his dynasty forever (2 Sam. 7).[14]

The story of Jehu's rebellion (2 Kgs 9–10) does not attempt to
dissociate him from the bloody deeds which brought him to power,
but rather endeavours to show that his acts were in compliance with
YHWH's will. Jehu is anointed by a prophet, indicating that it was the
divine will rather than personal ambition that motivated him. His
elimination of King Joram, Jezebel, and the potential heirs in
Samaria is each time accompanied by the citation of the prophecy of
Elijah against Ahab (2 Kgs 9.25-26, 36-37; 10.10, 17). His mass
slaughter of Baal worshippers is not specifically justified, but it
conforms to Biblical law. Jehu's alliance with Jonadab ben Rechub
shows the purity of his zeal for YHWH. The author or later editor
brings the account to a conclusion by recording a divine word of
approval for his actions, to be rewarded by four generations of his
dynasty on the throne (2 Kgs 10.30).[15]

The use of forensic narration in defense of persons in power is
occasionally dubbed 'propaganda' in recent literature.[16] We take that
to mean that the author sacrifices the truth to serve the cause of
legitimization. The potential is certainly there.[17] However, the mere
fact that persuasion is being employed in the service of royalty does
not disqualify the narrative's claim to truth. If the aim of persuasion
is *prima facie* evidence of falsehood, no judicial system can pretend to

justice. Since we have no independent access to the events rendered, we can only judge their truth on their historical, psychological and theological compellingness. That has been in fact the source of their impact on readers over the centuries.

The use of forensic narration to prosecute constitutes an even more fertile development and contributes the most profound images for Israelite self-consciousness. Here we find rhetorical situations which required the open, honest airing of unpleasant facts. These seem to have generated a tradition which shaped the consciousness of Israelite readers to such an extent that 'stiff-neckedness' became an expected character-trait and made further exposés easier to sell. Tracing down the original situations and the later appropriation of these unflattering narratives is the task we have set for the remainder of this chapter.

Corroborating God's Judgment

Narratives of offenses which end in a prophetic word of judgment against the offender are prime candidates for the classification of forensic narration. A story is told which explains and justifies the quasi-judicial event of prophecy. The narrative is not addressed to judges, but to the Israelite public in defense of the Judge's decision.[18]

Narratives of offenses followed by prophetic words of judgment are scattered through the Former and Latter Prophets. An unnamed man of God condemns the house of Eli for violations of cultic law (1 Sam. 2.12-17, 22-25, 27-36); Samuel twice disinherits Saul for disobeying (1 Sam. 13.8-15; 15.1-33); Nathan convicts David of murder and adultery (2 Sam. 11–12); an unnamed prophet judges the king of Israel for letting the Aramean king go free (1 Kgs 20.26-43); Elijah condemns Ahab for murdering Naboth and confiscating his property (1 Kgs 21.1-29) and Ahaziah for seeking healing from a Philistine deity (2 Kgs 1.2-4); and Amos confronts Amaziah over the freedom to prophesy (Amos 7.10-17).[19] There is such a similarity among these that one can say that they constitute something of a genre.

At the core of this 'genre' is the prophecy of judgment against individuals. It consists of a commission and messenger formula, and an accusation or indictment and sentence.[20] The prophet relays the decision of the divine judge. However, in our literature this genre of prophecy is embedded in narrative. The narrative explains the

purport of the prophecy. But it does more than that: It persuades the reader that the addressee of the prophecy was indeed guilty of a high crime or offense and warranted the divine condemnation. In other words, it functions as a forensic narration to the report of the divine verdict.

The prophecy of judgment against individuals can be classified as a supplementary judicial system. That is to say, the individuals singled out for judgment were kings or high officials who were 'immune' to the judgment of the human judiciary by virtue of their office. In some cases, too, the offenses committed were not judiciable: for instance, disobeying a prophet, trying to silence a prophet, or building an elaborate tomb. YHWH intervened where the human system of justice was incapable of acting.[21]

These judicial interventions of YHWH were of interest not only to the person concerned, but to the public at large. The persons condemned were public figures, and their condemnation was of great public consequence. This accounts, we think, for the remembrance of the prophet's word and the formation of a narrative around it to give it context and persuasive force.

The acquiescence of the people in the prophetic judgment would not have been automatic. As we know from the experience of the classical prophets, the people did not always accept the prophet's message as divinely authorized. When a king, who was hedged about with sanctity and identified with the nation, was condemned by a prophet, their natural reaction would have been to dismiss the prophet as some sort of dangerous radical. On the other hand, the readers may have heard rumors of the king's crimes and be open to persuasion. The narrator of these forensic accounts, who was invariably an apologist for the YHWH of the prophets, could exploit the reader's ambivalence, prick his or her conscience, and elicit concurrence in the divine verdict.

The narrator could employ the arts of the storyteller to add force to his persuasive argument. He could build a framework around the 'knowledge' of the event, which would have been chiefly in the form of rumor among all but those closest to the persons involved. If the historian had an insider's knowledge, he could use it to advantage. But he would also have built upon rumor, on the 'images' of the individuals in the public mind, and perhaps on prejudices as well. To substantiate the case against the addressee, he would have to dramatize the motives and designs of the persons involved, often through fictive monolog or dialog; perhaps incidents would have to

be invented as well to explain the connections between known occurrences.

Many of these accounts are very well crafted, and attract the commentary of literary critics. To what degree is their artfulness extrinsic to their rhetorical purpose, and to what degree intrinsic? This sort of question really cannot be answered from the evidence, for it is in part a philosophical issue. Sternberg considers the poetics of a piece to be a variable independent of its history and thought.[22] The authors sought to entertain and satisfy their audience as well as to instruct it. According to this idea, a simple report of the crime or offense would be sufficient for the rhetorical purpose, so that artful development was an extraneous factor.

We would, however, propose a closer link between art and rhetoric. The more difficult the job of persuasion—in cases like David, probably Ahab[23]—the more the story has to live in front of the reader's eyes, the more subtle must be the psychology, the more delicate the irony. On the other hand, when the person concerned was not attractive or important to the original audience, a bare report suffices.[24]

At a more philosophical level, we would argue that narrative art is not an adornment, but an essential aspect of what is communicated. What literary critics isolate for analysis is actually a constituent part of the truth the author has to tell. The authors communicate moral and metaphysical insight by the way they shape the reader's perception of the events narrated. Biblical theology itself employs the art of characterization and representation of action, for YHWH is not a concept, but a narratively rendered persona.[25]

The authors of these narratives succeeded not only in convincing the original audience of the guilt of the personages condemned by YHWH, they produced what might be called paradigmatic accounts of human sin and divine judgment. It is this power to capture the universal in the particular that made their stories live on and continue to teach long after the persons and their fates were of no practical concern to the reader. They did so well that the stories have etched themselves as deeply on the Western imagination as any in the tradition.

Two Case Studies

Our description of the genre needs to be applied to some specific cases. The tendency toward generality has been one of the problems

that has aroused opposition to form criticism.[26] The value of a classification must ultimately be assessed in terms of its illumination of particular pericopes. Can the classification of the narratives associated with prophecies against individuals explain their themes, point-of-view, and artistic shaping? Can it be used to evaluate their historical fidelity? Does it lead to any insights into the particular rhetorical situation of a given pericope?

We can begin with one of the most famous and powerful, the story of Naboth, Ahab and Jezebel, and the prophet Elijah (1 Kgs 21). The prophecy and narratives are fused so tightly together that one could not understand the extremely laconic accusation and sentence— 'Have you killed and also taken possession?. . . In the place where the dogs licked up the blood of Naboth shall dogs lick up your own blood'—without the narrative, and the narrative would offend the conscience without the intervention of YHWH.[27]

The narrative begins with Naboth's refusal of Ahab's offer to buy his land. Ahab's offer seems fair enough, so the narrator takes care to justify Naboth's refusal; his reply is short, but he appeals to a powerful value—the family inheritance—and casts his obligation to preserve it as a sacred trust. Ahab's reaction—sulking—is natural, if a bit infantile. The narrator must explain how this impotent tantrum is translated into a heinous crime. Jezebel is chosen, probably because of her image in the public (esp. loyal Yahwists') mind. She is a foreigner, patron of the Baal-Asherah cult, imbued with an ethic of royal supremacy, and an assertive woman. One can believe that she would do such a deed. There is a positive side to her which also motivates her to do it: She is solicitous of her husband's feelings. In a very unusual scene we see her writing letters to the elders of Jezreel commanding them to implement a plan of judicial murder. The plan and its execution are a bit puzzling—to honour Naboth, then charge him with blasphemy?[28] The judicial murder is recounted and reported five times, providing the narrator's view, then the conspirator's report, then Jezebel's perception and her report to Ahab, then his perception. If one reads closely, it becomes clear that Jezebel hides the crime from Ahab and he does not want to know how Naboth died.

When Elijah is introduced, it is in such a way that the impression is conveyed that he knew nothing of these events until YHWH reveals them to him. His knowledge is supernatural, and therefore unimpeachable. Our judgment, shaped by the forensic narrative, is confirmed

by divine revelation, and our sense of justice is satisfied by the divine intervention.

Any follow-up to this prophecy would appear anti-climactic, but the story does continue. The conversation that ensues between Ahab and Elijah (vv. 20-24) does not fit the story well. It assumes that Ahab is such an evil character that he is too hardened to feel the pangs of conscience, though the narrative has led us to believe that he really did not directly instigate the crime and might not have gone along willingly. Elijah is in character but out of situation, setting the fate of Ahab and his dynasty in the broader contexts of history as though he had become the historian. Ahab's repentance and YHWH's compassionate postponement of the sentence (vv. 27-29) are somewhat more fitting.[29]

Our passage must have been written when the fate of Ahab and the Omride dynasty was of direct interest to the people of the northern kingdom. The narrative carefully reports the crimes for which he is condemned, shaping the incidents and dialog to show how a sulking king became guilty through the conspiracy of his imperious and unscrupulous queen with some compliant city fathers and worthless thugs. The narrative may have originated in the wake of the prophecy itself, while Ahab was still living, or it may have originated in the subsequent decade of the dynasty's reign, or at the latest during the reign of Jehu, whose bloody overthrow of the Omrides was justified as punishment for this crime (see 2 Kgs 9.25-26, 36-37).[30] After Jehu, Ahab's legitimacy was out of the question; he had become the epitome of unrighteous and apostate rule.

How much did the author of the forensic narration know? The answer must be conjectural, but we can set the outer limits. He knew Elijah's prophecy, with its indictment of Ahab for murder and the confiscating of Naboth's property. He probably knew that Ahab had tried to buy the land, and Naboth had refused. He also knew that Naboth had died by stoning for a crime of which he had been falsely charged, and that soon afterward Ahab had shown up on the premises. Everything else is probably supposition and invention. He could not have known that Jezebel instigated the crime, and he probably had no firm evidence that the elders of Jezreel were complicit. But Jezebel was easy to pin the blame on; there may have already been a rumor circulating about her role. As to the role of the elders, it is 'logical' to assume that at least a few carried out the plan at the behest of the king or queen.

The account of David's adultery and murder (2 Sam. 11-12) exhibits consummate artistry, and has been the subject of imaginative and powerful readings by two recent literary critics.[31] It is striking that neither reading makes much of the structural and rhetorical linkage of the narrative to Nathan's parable and prophecy. This is the clue to the narrative's rhetorical force. The beloved David is being convicted of heinous crimes. The author must overcome the strong resistance to this revelation. He carefully portrays the sequence of events to show how David got in deeper and deeper, against his will and good sense. His adultery with Bathsheba was blameworthy, but understandable in persons of power. His attempt to cover it up led to the almost comic game played between him and Uriah, whose loyalty and integrity prove beyond reproach, even if he did know what the king was up to.[32] David's desire to cover up then crossed over into the conspiracy. Joab exculpates himself of the matter and David accepts the responsibility.

Notice how reserved the author has been regarding the thoughts and motives of all the parties in the story. This is unusual for forensic narration, for the legal classification of the acts includes foreknowledge and intention. In this narrative, the reader is not directly informed of these; rather, we are expected to fill them in. Though this might be considered a rhetorical defect, it really is the opposite. That David's actions were criminal is never in doubt; the reader is allowed to recreate the workings of his mind, and of Bathsheba's and Uriah's as well, in order to exercise some type of judgment in the process of coming to comprehend YHWH's verdict. In addition, the author was able to maintain a respectful silence about the mind and heart of a beloved monarch.

David himself was evidently on the narrator's side, for he responds to Nathan's prophecy by admitting his crime and seeking divine mercy. The conclusion, which allowed the restoration of the king to legitimacy, also brought the reluctant reader to admit his guilt.[33]

When was this account written? Literary critics differ on whether the forensic narration and prophecy belong to the author of the 'throne succession narrative' (2 Sam. 13.20; 1 Kgs 1-2).[34] If the present account belongs to that longer work, as seems to be the case, then it can be dated in relation to the rhetorical situation that occasioned the story of Solomon's succession to the throne. Since that narrative is designed to exonerate Solomon of any crimes in the disposal of Adonijah and his supporters,[35] it must have been written

when such deeds represented a threat to his legitimacy, viz., early in his reign.

Those who separate the account from the throne succession narrative, though, have a point in their favor. The account of David's crimes in association with Solomon's origins is not an obvious support of Solomon's royal legitimacy. The prophecy and some forensic narration must have preceded the Solomonic apologetic and virtually forced itself on the author of the latter. This earlier account would be dated sometime in David's reign, perhaps at the time of Absolom's rebellion (cf. 2 Sam. 12.11-12).

What did the author know of the events that led to Nathan's prophecy of judgment against David? That David committed adultery with Bathsheba and engineered Uriah's death in the Ammonite war must have been public knowledge after Nathan's prophecy. Much of the story of Uriah's visit may have been invented; possibly, though, it was a fictively transformed rendition of rumors deriving from David's bodyguard, which plays a rather prominent role in the story.

Our general classification appears to be confirmed by the foregoing application to two particular, salient examples. The narratives which accompany propecies of judgment against Ahab and David exhibit the forensic shaping of the story of their actions. Their purpose would appear to be to convince the audience of the guilt of the addressee and the justice of the divine intervention. The narrator wove together public knowledge and rumor, and perhaps some insider's knowledge at times, with supposition and invention, to set forth the deeds condemned by YHWH.

Theological Apologetic and Dynastic Politics

One narrative appears to have a distinctive apologetic motive. Meir Sternberg has shown convincingly that 1 Samuel 15 is crafted as an apology for YHWH's rejection of Saul. The divine condemnation of Saul for violating the spirit and the letter of his command to exterminate the Amalekites was potentially capable of arousing sympathy for Saul, so the narrator crafted the dialog to show that Saul was not a good king, that he exercised weak leadership and was willing to pass the blame to the people to save his own neck. The judgment of the readers, thus, should converge with YHWH's stricter standards.[36]

Sternberg's argument can be generalized. All of the examples of forensic narration have the purpose of convincing the reader of the truth and justice of YHWH's judgments. The case of Saul may be a bit more complex than most of the others—hence the extended exchange between prophet and king—but all are seeking the same general effect. Our narrators are endeavouring to 'defend' the God of the prophets.

Why would this be necessary? One may surmise that Yahwism was always forced to persuade Israel of its truth. YHWH's claims upon the nation's mind and heart were frequently in jeopardy; the common people and even the rulers, priests and wisemen were natural assimilationists, so the national religion was regularly threatened with syncretism. The prophets were the spokesmen for a militant Yahwism, representing probably only a minority of the total populace. It was the prophets and their supporters who not only pronounced judgment but also endeavoured to persuade the people of YHWH's truth and righteousness. Our narratives, and much of Biblical literature, is a by-product of their apologetic.

Their writings, however, were not untouched by the politics of the national (and local) institutions. We must consider the possibility that they were used in various causes. The narrative Sternberg treats of Saul's condemnation, for example, has been preserved as an apologetic for David as well. Samuel leaves the encounter with Saul to anoint a successor from the house of Jesse (1 Sam. 16.1-13). The author who constructed this sequence felt that the narrative which told of Saul's reign and David's ascent to power needed to be bolstered. Although this narrative—or at least the extant narrative of 1 Samuel 8–2 Samuel 5—supports the legitimacy of David, it leaves a residual sympathy for Saul. Saul, indeed, borders on a tragic hero, a person arbitrarily rejected and hounded to death by YHWH. YHWH's decision and David's legitimacy needed further corroboration.

It is possible that the crime of Ahab and Jezebel was recreated as an apology for Jehu; it certainly was used by Jehu to justify his brutal annihilation of the Omride dynasty and its collaborators (2 Kgs 9–10). The more likely scenario is that the forensic narration ending in the prophecy of Elijah against Ahab originated during Ahab's reign and fueled an underground resistance to his policies (political as well as religious) among loyal Yahwists. Jehu was probably a product of that environment and thought of himself as purifying the nation of Omride depredations.

If the prophetic narratives were composed and/or disseminated by usurping dynasties, they were a double-edged sword. If YHWH judges one's predecessor, he could always judge him or his successors. One's apologia was a potential noose. A distinctly anti-absolutist view of monarchy thereby took shape in the tradition. The king ruled at the pleasure of YHWH, and YHWH was quite capable of bringing him to judgment via the prophets. The people who read these narratives as their national history gained a critical attitude toward the behavior of human rulers, aware that power corrupts its wielders, who must be held in check by the Ruler of history.

Corroborating National Judgment

The forensic narrations did not cease to communicate to audiences after they served their original purposes. They are preserved for us because they were found to have an enduring relevance to those who recognized YHWH as their God. The task of this section is to trace the meaning they had for later generations, culminating in their incorporation into the Deuteronomistic History,[37] whose story is a forensic narration on a grand scale.

The accounts of offenses by kings and high officials obviously lost their immediate relevance when the perpetrators passed from the scene. The offender had been brought to justice. In the case of David, the crime had been forgiven and the dynasty remained legitimate. After Solomon, the scope of its claim was reduced to Judah, so the story of David would have had a different meaning for southerners than northerners. For southerners, the story forcefully underscored its kingship's dependence on YHWH's unmerited favor for its legitimacy.

The story of David's offense, along with the narratives of his rise to power and the tragedies of his reign, checked a desire on the part of Judeans to idealize the founder of the dynasty and the age during which he ruled. Evidence of this idealization creeps into the otherwise realistic Deuteronomistic History in the recurring statements about David's integrity and righteousness (1 Kgs 9.4; 11.4, 6, 33; 14.8; 15.3, 5, 11; 2 Kgs 14.3; 16.2; 18.3; 22.2).[38] The idealization culminates in the Davidic history in 1 Chronicles, which virtually eliminates all evidence of the darker side of his story.

The other accounts of prophetic condemnations do not concern figures on whom institutional legitimacy continued to depend. Once the Omri dynasty was usurped by Jehu, readers had no investment in

the status of Ahab and Ahaziah. In fact, the tradition highlighted their dark side, indicating the illegitimacy of the entire dynasty. The Deuteronomistic Historian says of Ahab: 'Indeed there was never anyone like Ahab, who committed himself to doing what was displeasing to the LORD at the instigation of his wife Jezebel' (1 Kgs 21.25). At the same time, the prophets of YHWH—Elijah, Micaiah and Elisha—are depicted as the champions of truth and wielders of power. We might even say that the Omrides were remembered because they were the targets of prophetic words and acts.

Each account seems to have had its own rhetorical history; however, there must have been a certain generalizing impact in the very recurrence. When king after king and official after official were subjected to YHWH's judgment, Israel would have learned to take a critical attitude toward persons in high places. Whatever the official ideology of kingship and priesthood, the people became aware of repeated conflict between YHWH and those who claimed to represent him. The YHWH of the prophets was more frequently at odds with his official representatives—kings and priests—than in harmony with them.

This perception culminates in the Deuteronomistic Historian's grading of the kings of Israel and Judah. Every northern king is condemned as having 'done evil in the sight of YHWH, provoking Him to anger',[39] and only a few Judean kings escape a similar judgment. Admittedly, his criteria of judgment, particularly his condemnation of 'the sins of Jeroboam ben Nebat'—his sanctuaries in Bethel and Dan with their 'calf images'—are somewhat *ex post facto*; but he also assembled prophetic accounts of judgment to substantiate his accusations.[40] The reader of his history cannot but come away with a dismal view of royal behavior.

Down through the history of interpretation since canonization, these accounts of crimes and offenses in high places have been applied to political and ecclesiastic officials. Readers have been taught to measure rulers against divine standards of justice and piety, and to expect that power will corrupt those who possess it. Particular cases which occurred now and again in Israel's history became heuristic images for all times and places.

These stories of divine judgment of official wrongdoing, however, had national import as well. There is a natural identification between a people and their kings. The king is the symbol and instrument of the national mind and will. The king's victories are the people's victories; his defeats theirs. When a king is brought before the bar of

divine judgment, the people might be relieved to have an oppressor or bad leader removed and the nation restored to health. Nevertheless, the people were sufficiently identified with their rulers that they could not help but be uneasy. When ruler after ruler came under YHWH's prophetic scrutiny, the cumulative effect would be to sense a national scope to the guilt. When the prophets of communal judgment made their appearance,[41] the people surely recognized their message to be an extension of the judgments they had witnessed.

These forensic narrations seem to have had the capacity to thematize a tacit knowledge on the part of the general populace of something wrong in the national character. The sacred story by which they understood themselves was, in a sense, incomplete; in it YHWH was Israel's deliverer, the source of its law and institutions, the fountain of blessings and the source of its power. Israel had been chosen by YHWH to be his own special possession, and their destiny was to be glorious. Only on the margins were there hints of a 'dark side', of the obtuseness of the people and its rulers, and the difficulties and disappointments at home and on the international scene. The prophetic word gave them a way to understand these 'gaps' in the self-understanding provided by the sacred tradition.

The Deuteronomistic Historian preserves the accounts of wrongdoing in high places as an integral part of the case he is making for Israel's rebellion against YHWH, and YHWH's justice in destroying the nation and sending the survivors into exile.[42] One can understand the entire Deuteronomistic History as an extended forensic narration, built up of these forensic narrations and other accounts which tended, cumulatively, toward the same point. When we classify the Deuteronomistic History as a forensic narration, we have extended the analogy one step further. The narrator is not weaving together evidence known to the public of a specific offense, but compiling records, written accounts, and perhaps oral traditions into a cumulative case for national judgment. The reader is no longer only the 'judge' of the justice of YHWH's judgment of someone else, but the 'accused'—a member of the people which must acknowledge its guilt and the justice of divine judgment.

We have what amounts to a *confirmatio* in 2 Kgs 17.7-23. After reporting the destruction of the northern kingdom and the exile of its inhabitants, the author offers an explanation. The people of Israel had persisted in rebellion against YHWH, though he had been gracious to them and provided a law to guide them. They knew their

duty, but did not perform it. But YHWH did not condemn them immediately; he kept warning them by prophets. Finally he ran out of patience and removed them from his sight.

Why did the historian step outside the narrative framework to deliver this argument? He had foreshadowed the course of things to come in Deut. 29.1–30.10 and the poetic prophecy in Deuteronomy 32, and again in the last words of Joshua (Josh. 23; 24); he drove home the tenor of his theme in his assessment of each king's performance, his interpolations into the words of the prophets, and his selection and arrangement of incidents. In 2 Kings 17, he 'adds up the ledger', so to speak. In place of a prophecy he lets the event of divine judgment itself stand, interpreted in his own words.[43] The reader cannot escape the conclusion that YHWH was justified in his judgment, his people were amply prepared for it, and they should now accept the blame.

The author makes his appeal to his audience in the addresses of Moses at the beginning of his work, the book of Deuteronomy. Here we find what might be called condensed cumulative forensic narrations. The Song of Moses (Deut. 32), which has been entitled a 'covenant *rîb*' by some scholars,[44] rehearses the history of God's people from its election by YHWH, through the centuries of apostasy, to divine punishment. The 'prophecy' of Moses provides the reader with the divine perspective on the course of events to follow and thus validates the historian's conclusions in 2 Kings 17.

It may be worth noting that the Song of Moses is an example of a genre of cumulative forensic narration which occurs in the Psalter[45] and in the books of the classical prophets. In the prophecies of communal judgment, we find a distinctive group which goes beyond a series of accusations to recount the history of YHWH and his people.[46] The gracious actions of YHWH are set in contrast to the apostasy and injustice of the people, with the incongruity spelling judgment.[47] This type of narration serves to connect the accusations logically and dramatically to the sentence. The audience is forced to grasp the incongruity of the nation's story and concur in the decision of YHWH to judge it.

The Deuteronomistic Historian had only to transpose this type of poetic cumulative forensic narration into a prose narrative of the national history. The Song of Moses links the prose composition to the poetic tradition behind it. Though the Deuteronomistic Historian never actually records a prophecy of national judgment in his

narrative,[48] he recruits that tradition in support of his argument by means of this Mosaic forensic narration.

The classical prophets spoke before the event, the Deuteronomistic Historian after it.[49] The prophets were seeking to persuade their audience to agree with YHWH's decision and either repent in time or undergo the punishment appropriately. The Historian is seeking to persuade the remnant—who are now 'exile'[50]—to concur in YHWH's judgment in order to learn from it. Although the story the Historian has to tell ends in judgment, his purpose is to elicit repentance.

There are a number of indications that this is the rhetorical effect he seeks. The Song of Moses does not end with the judgment of the people of God; it passes on to the vindication of God's people in the judgment of the nations (Deut. 32.34-43). There is hope for the nation in exile. In Moses' address in Deut. 29-30, he warns of the consequences of forsaking the covenant with YHWH; then he continues beyond that dreaded event:

> When all these things befall you—the blessing and the curse that I have set before you—and you take them to heart amidst the various nations to which the LORD your God has banished you, and you return to the LORD your God, and you and your children heed His command with all your heart and soul, just as I enjoin upon you this day, then the LORD your God will restore your fortunes and take you back in love. He will bring you together again from all the peoples where the LORD your God has scattered you.

Here, certainly, we get a glimpse into the historical situation the author understands himself to be speaking to and a straightforward statement of how the story should be appropriated.[51]

The ending of the Deuteronomistic History is consonant with this rhetorical setting. We might have expected a *confirmatio* for the exile of Judah comparable to that for Israel. Instead, the author leaves it for the reader to make this application (hinted at in 2 Kgs 17.19-20). The events leading to exile are simply recounted (2 Kgs 24-25). The moment foretold in Deut. 30.1ff. has arrived; the reader should understand how to respond. The author even leaves the reader with a glimmer of hope: Jehoiachin's release from prison in Babylon to sit among the kings of the Empire.

This rhetorical situation too passed, and the Deuteronomistic History entered into new and different relationships with audiences. Though these transactions are largely hidden from our sight, it is still

possible to observe a particular stamp that the work put on the Jews of subsequent generations. It shaped the consciousness of the reader to understand him- or herself as an exile. 'Exile', *galut*, became and has until modern times remained the symbol of the condition of the people of God.[52] The books of the prophets of judgment and subsequent events—particularly the destruction of the Temple in 70 CE—confirmed and reinforced this self-understanding, but it seems certain that the Deuteronomistic History was the prime mover.

Some exiles did return and rebuild the city and temple. The History could have been continued, but unlike the Chronicler's work it was left in exile. The *Tradenten* must have grasped that it would have enervated the rhetorical force of the work to continue. The full hopes of the book, and of the prophets, were not realized in the restoration; only an event of eschatological proportions would do so.[53] Hence, the Deuteronomistic History's call to repentance in exile in the hope of a glorious and transformative redemption was allowed to echo from generation to generation.

We have followed the rhetorical exchange of a set of passages from their origins in particular political contexts through to their universalization as representations of the enduring conflict between those in power and the sovereign God, and as testimony to the cumulative guilt of the people of God. The author who has preserved them shaped his entire work as a comprehensive forensic narration designed to persuade the Judean exiles to acknowledge the justice of YHWH's judgment and to return to Him with a whole heart and soul. We who read this work are conditioned to understand ourselves as living in exile, between the times, called to take this story to heart and redeem the time.

Conclusions

The case has been made for identifying a set of passages within the Former and Latter Prophets, and the whole Deuteronomistic History, as forensic narration. In the accounts of crimes and offenses committed by high officials, the narrator wove together the known or rumored facts into a story which convicted the addressee of the prophecy of judgment. These accounts were universalized by later readers into representative examples of the abuse of power and into evidence for the judgment of the whole people of God. The Deuteronomistic Historian incorporated them in a forensic narrative covering the history of Israel from settlement to exile, a work whose

desired rhetorical effect was to convince the Judean exiles to concur in God's judgment and repent.

The rhetorical classification of forensic narration is not intended to cover all Biblical narratives. Others may fall under epideictic, deliberative or some other classification not recognized in classical rhetoric. Most of the stories in the Pentateuch, and in Joshua and Judges, do not seem to be guided by the purpose of ascribing innocence or guilt to the personages involved. At most, the guilt of the Pharaoh and his people is a secondary motif in the exodus, and the accounts of battles for control of Canaan do not involve a judicial perspective. While law and judicial enforcement are frequently in the background of the sacred history, only occasionally do we find forensic narration to be dominant.

There is a set of stories with a distinctive judicial cast, the 'murmuring' or rebellion of the people in the wilderness.[54] These do appear to be designed to persuade the reader that the people, or some party, were guilty in the sight of YHWH. It is not clear, though, that they are, like the forensic narrations in the Former and Latter Prophets, based upon publicly known facts. They may have been fabricated to provide evidence that even in the sacred past, Israel's national character exhibited its rebellious side. However, one cannot dismiss the possibility that memories of discontent and rebellion were embedded in the tradition. The authors may have treated these vague memories the way they did the rumors about crimes in high places, weaving them into accounts designed to persuade the reader of the guilt and innocence of the parties involved.

This chapter has demonstrated the potential value of using classical rhetorical categories in the interpretation of Biblical literature. In some cases our results confirmed the judgment of critical scholars who were operating without the aid of classical rhetoric; in others we grasped passages in new ways. Bringing them under a common classification should augment our knowledge and produce further insight. In the process, we have justified the use of the term 'history' for these narratives and even found a basis for assessing their fidelity to the events they record.

PART II

Chapter 5

FINDING THE BEST JOB

There is a tension in the program we are proposing for Biblical interpretation. On the one hand, we argue that a text communicates transactionally. That is, the author and audience 'negotiate' its meaning together. The author works within the conventions and perceptual horizon of his or her imagined audience to have a certain effect; even in the original transaction, though, the interests and perceptions of the audience will differ sufficiently from the author's to alter the meaning subtly from what the author had in mind. When the text enters a tradition, subsequent audiences will be somewhat removed from the conventions and shared understanding of the original transaction, and new interests and expectations will guide what they receive from the text. Each transaction through history realizes some possible meaning of the text and has had some effect on its interpreters. To cite a rabbinic proverb, 'God intends all the meanings that He has made us capable of discovering (in His word)'.[1]

On the other hand, we believe that a serious interpretive strategy requires the capacity to judge good from poor (or even perverse) interpretations. Whether one is studying the history of interpretation, or engaging in exegesis of a Biblical text, one needs to be able to assess how well the construal of the text fits the words and the subject matter. If one wants to learn as much from the text as possible, it is necessary to have norms or criteria for judging whether a text says what interpreters find in it.

The challenge is to reconcile the affirmation of the potential value of all interpretations with the commitment to norms of exegetical performance. We cannot allow either conviction to overpower the other, nor can we accommodate them by separating their functions. Rather, the two must interact productively with one another.

An Abortive Reconciliation

It will be worth looking briefly at a typical but faulty way of combining a normative understanding of textual meaning with the history of interpretation. In the Postscript to an anthology of some thirty-two different interpretations of the book of Job, Nahum Glatzer observes that 'the book of Job was recreated by its interpreters in their own image—with a few notable exceptions—both in times past and in the current era'.[2] Although he might have said that this is as it should be, that communication requires receivers to assimilate a text into their conceptual and affective world, he considers such assimilation to be a prime source of interpretative error. When the text of Job is made over into the image of the interpreters, it serves 'the purpose of shielding humanity against its harsh impact'.[3] Perhaps, now, though, having seen the translation of Job into various interpreters' modes of thinking and the adaptation of it to their needs, we can read and interpret it according to what 'the original Job drama intended to convey'.[4] 'Then the literal meaning will of necessity replace allegory, transposition, and reformulation, and "text" and "interpretation" will coincide.'[5]

Glatzer's view of what a true interpretation is and how it is achieved ignores the transactional character of textual meaning, and therefore projects an impossible and undesirable ideal for the interpreter to emulate. If the ideal interpretation of Job must be a perfectly disinterested one, Glatzer himself would fail, for he believes that his own unbiased, unflinching interpretation constitutes a message dearly needed by our secular, scientific age.[6] Such an appeal is a sure sign of an interested interpreter, one who is assimilating a text to the intellectual and affective horizon of the receiving community. Moreover, his claim to be able to achieve the literal meaning, as opposed to those corrupted by devious interpretive devices, is calculated to persuade a secular, scientific audience of its truth.

It is not in principle illegitimate for Glatzer to assimilate the text to the mindset of his audience, but he has contradicted his own explicit and implicit convictions about truth in interpretation. The lesson to draw from his failure is that disinterestedness is an impossible ideal. The modern critical scholar does not have a privileged access to the true meaning of a text, for critical method does not free the interpreter from his or her interests or attain some

timeless perspective on textual meaning. The pity is that critical scholars claim privileged access and arrogantly dismiss precritical interpretation as fraudulent.

Not only is the ideal of scholarly detachment impossible to attain, it is undesirable. The personal or existential component of this understanding may not be very prominent when the text is a 'laundry list' dug up in an archaeological excavation, but it certainly plays a decisive role in the interpretation of a profound religious work like Job. The capacity of the interpreter to recognize the subject of the drama as a subject of concern to the interpreter enhances its power to communicate. A truly detached reader would learn virtually nothing about what the text has to say and would remain untouched by the reading.

The greatness of the book of Job consists in its capacity to elicit an 'existential struggle' in the reader with the mystery of evil and suffering. When readers interpret Job, they invariably work out their own understanding of the human condition. The book has the density and opaqueness of human existence itself, so it is not surprising that it has generated an array of interpretations practically as diverse as the world views generated by the experience of living.

The fecundity of the book of Job is a virtue, not a defect. It has yielded meaning to generation upon generation of readers. If it were not as susceptible to diverse readings, it would not have been capable of speaking so profoundly and provocatively to the various conditions of humanity.

The Need for Norms of Judgment

This celebration of pluralism can go only so far, though. We cannot float around among possible world views and still take our existence seriously. Likewise, an interpreter cannot simply entertain the possibilities of understanding that have arisen in the history of interpretation, but must take up the task of grasping the book of Job as a coherent work of art and theology. We must take our stand among competing interpretations in order to make sense of it for ourselves and our contemporaries, just as our predecessors did for themselves and their generations.

How are we to be guided in our interpretation? It may sound outrageous, but we propose that the interpreter be guided by his or her personal concerns. The drama of Job requires the interpreter's engagement in its question to communicate all that it has to say and

move the interpreter most profoundly. Serious interpretation of this work involves a confluence of the text's subject and the interpreter's concerns.[7] Glatzer is right that historically interpreters have assimilated the book to their own horizon and interests, or as he puts it, 'recreated (it)... in their own image'. This is as it should be.

However, one must distinguish between interpretations which learn from the text and those which dominate it. It should be self-evident that the ideal interpreter seeks to learn from the text rather then to use it to confirm and propagate what he or she already knows. If the text renders a world we potentially or actually share, or sets forth an argument we are willing to adopt, our own thinking is deepened and broadened in proportion to how well we listen to and even 'strengthen'[8] the text. If it opposes us, we should state the strongest case against ourselves and thereby strengthen our own thinking.

The same point can be cast in affective terms as well. A text seeks to move us as well as communicate to the mind. If the text has the power to grip us, it is important that it arouse what is most noble and righteous in us, not what is base and self-aggrandizing. The very commitment to listening to what the text has to say subdues the interpreter's will to dominate, rendering one free to consider other perspectives and be moved by them. In opening oneself to the text, the interpreter should 'strengthen' the text by responding to that which ennobles rather than that which debases.

The Aesthetic Hypothesis

This portrait of legitimate or ideal interpretation can be captured in a normative principle. The philosopher Ronald Dworkin has proposed what he calls the 'aesthetic hypothesis' to describe what literary critics are disagreeing about when they debate competing interpretations of a work. He formulates his hypothesis in these words: 'An interpretation of a piece of literature attempts to show which way of reading... the text reveals it as the best work of art'.[9] Although Dworkin formulates this as a description of actual practice, it appears to be a norm against which interpretations can be judged. Hence it could just as well be formulated as a dictum: Interpret a text in the way that reveals it as the best work of art. The principle also appears to be expandable, so that not only the aesthetic but the intellectual and affective values of the text are included. The

expanded formulation could run: Interpret a text as the best text (aesthetically, intellectually and affectively) the text can be.

The dictum strikes the balance we are looking for between the subjective and objective components of interpretation. On the one hand, a text is a determinate entity. It consists of specific words in a specific language from a specific moment in history. The language has not only lexical and grammatical form, it also passes on idioms, associations and genres which shape the formation of a given work and its reception by an audience. Each work embodies these generic structures, and to understand it the scholarly reader must know or reconstruct them. The dictum grants the text integrity, even priority, in the interpretive act; the interpreter should seek the best text *it can be*, not the text he or she desires it to be.

On the other hand, a text is more than an artifact; it is a communication. The structured whole must be received by a reader. This introduces a certain indeterminacy into its meaning. This subjective aspect of interpretation is preserved in the dictum's words, 'best text'. What is 'best' is a judgment of the interpreter, involving his or her knowledge and values, social location and interests, and any other factor that might enter into the judgment as to what would make for a good text.

Criteria for Judging Interpretations
Before we demonstrate the usefulness of this dictum by applying it to the interpretation of Job, it may be worth our while to identify some of the criteria which might be employed to judge whether an interpreter reads a work as the best it can be. Two of the ones we are suggesting—comprehensiveness and consistency—derive from the way interpreters discuss the merits and defects of a line of interpretation; the remaining three are implicit in the rhetorical conception of the text.

Comprehensiveness. When we are dealing with an official or canonical text (i.e., a fixed block of language), an interpretation must take the whole work into account. It is axiomatic among interpreters to regard a proposed line of interpretation as unviable if significant portions of the work do not fit it well. It is a prerogative of an interpreter to focus on selected passages as keys to a work, but every word and sentence should find a place within the overall thesis.[10]

Consistency. An interpretation of a work must avoid internal

contradictions, shifting premises, arbitrary thematic changes, and so forth. It is an interpretive maxim that any serious logical incoherence or conceptual oscillation renders an interpretation unviable. Consistency is essential to intelligible and intelligent discourse.

Not only should interpretation be consistent, it should endeavor to find the work itself consistent. Since incoherence is fatal to an argument, a work which seeks to establish some proposition by argument would be a better work if it were coherent. Likewise, a narrative or drama will be a better work if characters remain in character, the action follows an inevitable course and reaches an appropriate resolution, and the perspective remains intelligible. The interpretation committed to grasping the text as the best text it can be will seek to discover how a work hangs together.

What about defective works of art or argumentation? Obviously one of the tasks of interpretation is criticism. If the efforts to discern consistency fail, the interpreter should diagnose the defect and perhaps 'reconstruct' the project imaginatively to remedy it.[11] The critic, though, should exercise humility, for the detection of flaws may actually be his or her failure to discern what makes the work hang together.

Cogency. An interpretation of a passage or work should, other things being equal, be the most natural or public way of construing it. An interpretation may be comprehensive and internally consistent, yet still not seem right. We may call it 'forced' or 'over-refined'. Such judgments are often hard to explain, but it is an important factor in assessing the value of an interpretation. An interpretation which construes the language of the work in its public sense, its genre among those which could be recognized by the readership for which it was composed, is superior to one which does not. Perhaps one has to take recourse to speculation at times: How would the original audience have most naturally taken this piece, given what we know of their language, oral and literary genres etc.? One should assume that the author knew his or her language, genre, cultural tradition and audience and was capable of achieving the effect he or she intended.

This applies to the original transaction more than to the transactions with subsequent audiences. How do we assess later interpretations? To understand the history of interpretation, one must be able to enter into the perspectives of the interpreters; in particular, to recreate the questions they were asking the text. Then

one must judge whether a given question was a germane and productive one, and assess whether the means by which the interpreter found an answer allowed the text to teach them anything.

How would we assess the cogency of our own interpretation? As we asked of earlier interpreters, we must ask ourselves whether the questions we are asking are germane and productive. If one decides that a piece is, say, a poor argument for a particular principle or policy, one should explore alternative possibilities which would make it a work with greater intellectual or affective force. To assess our method of answering our questions, we should use the rule that an interpretation most available to the general reader is preferable to an esoteric one. If the author was effective as a communicator, the text should continue to exhibit that power.[12]

Plenitude. This principle is only relevant to texts which have achieved the status of classics and have been interpreted from generation to generation. An interpretation is better if we can discern some insight in every, or practically every, moment of its interpretive history. The meaning of a classical text cannot be reduced to the author's intent[13] or the original exchange between author and audience; rather, it has a cumulative meaning—a meaning that incorporates all that it has meant. An interpretation that is reductive, that is, that says the work can only mean what it meant for some specific audience, or can only mean some particular thing for the contemporary audience, should be rejected for its imperialistic claims.

One should not, however, take up the interpretive ideal of a plenitude of meaning apart from the other criteria which have been enumerated. The interpreters of the past were fallible, so the interpreter must exercise judgment in the appropriation of past insights. One must measure every interpretation by the tests of comprehensiveness, consistency and cogency, in order to determine whether this possible meaning of the text enriches our own understanding of it.

Profundity. This is the most subjective criterion of all. However, it will and should play a part in deciding what interpretation makes the text the best text it can be. The interpreter must choose the interpretation which, other things being equal, makes the text the most profound understanding of its subject that the interpreter can envisage. Only so can the interpreter learn from the text, and if the interpreter is profound what he or she learns from the text will be of

great value to the interpretive community. If the interpreter is shallow, only shallow minds will take it seriously.

Interpreting Job

In the remainder of this chapter we will demonstrate the usefulness of the aesthetic hypothesis in the interpretation of Job. Our strategy will be to locate some of the problems that confront an interpreter, survey the views of past interpreters, and exhibit how the best text criterion can guide the exegete in making a proper judgment. It is not our purpose of to offer solutions, and such will be only briefly sketched now and then to illustrate how the dictum can be applied.

Deciding on the Text to be Interpreted

Job is one of those texts about which little can be taken for granted. To be sure, there is a fixed configuration of Hebrew words upon the pages, but there are a number of disputes over what to do about them. The upshot of the matter is, the interpreter must create the text to be interpreted.

The difficulties begin with the language itself. The book has an odd vocabulary, and probably more *hapax legomena* than any Old Testament writing. One must take recourse to Aramaic, and perhaps Ugaritic and Arabic, to recover the meaning of these lexical units. Moreover, the grammar is often sufficiently obscure to leave the reader in doubt as to what is being said.

Up to a point, these are technical issues to be solved by the best science of language at our disposal. There are debates between philologists regarding what the best science of language is,[14] but that has only an indirect bearing on how to interpret Job. One would not argue for one or another position in philology because it would make for a better understanding of Job.

Beyond the technical issues, though, there are decisions regarding the construal of statements in the book. We may agree on the meaning of the words and grammar, and still disagree on how to 'translate' them.[15] For example, the Rabbinic tradition tended to tone down Job's accusations against God, and indeed to eliminate as many as possible.[16] The interpreters endeavoured to read the Job of the dramatic poem as being as consistent with the pious figure of the prolog as the text would bear. They did have to grant that he

occasionally broke the bounds of proper piety, but these were in the way of 'slips', not persistent behavior.

Modern translators, on the other hand, have tended to construe Job's utterances in the dramatic poem as being as harsh and offensive as the language will bear. Where a statement could be a general complaint or dark rumination, it should be taken—according to this position—as being as specific and pointed as the linguistic configuration will allow. This trend in translation is informed by a view that the dramatic poem stands in severe tension with the prose prolog: it portrays a promethean Job in contrast to the conventionally pious figure of the prolog.

The dictum, to interpret Job as the best work it can be, can be brought to bear on the issue of translation. Does the translation which preserves as consistent a Job as possible produce a better work—artistically and theologically—than one which sets two quite different Jobs in opposition or juxtaposition to each other? Does the 'conservative' interpretation preserve a consistency in the characterization of Job within the dramatic poem? Does it account for the vehement reaction of Job's three companions? Does it make sense of the theophany and response?

Note that the questions of translation press the interpreter to answer questions at other levels of interpretation as well. Though one obviously has to be able to read the text before deciding what it is about, there is a 'feedback loop' in which the judgment as to what the book is about requires revision of the translation.

The relationship of the prose prolog to the dramatic poem is an important ingredient in translation. That opens up the question of 'sources'. Is the book the product of one author or many? If it is the product of more than one, should the interpreter try to locate the 'original work' and concentrate on it, or interpret the work in its extant, composite form?

Let us pursue the question of the relationship of the prose prolog and epilog (chs. 1–2; 42.7ff.) to the dramatic poem. Did the author of the dramatic poem compose the prose prolog and epilog? Is the poem intended to be read with the prolog and epilog (if he did not compose it)? If the dramatic poem was intended to be read as a part of the prose story, how should the relationship be construed? Does the perspective remain the same or does it change beginning in ch. 3? Does Job continue 'not to sin or blame God' (1.22)? If he does 'blame God', has he fallen from grace? Does the issue of the dramatic poem continue to be the testing of Job?

Within the poem there are also some source problems. Paramount among these is the appearance and address of Elihu. He appears out of nowhere and then disappears again after his one long address (chs. 33–37). His address follows the tenor of Job's three companions, though it may offer new wrinkles.[17] It interrupts what appears to be a natural connection between Job's challenge to God and God's response. Does the Elihu speech belong to the original dramatic poem or has it been interpolated?

Of another order is the apparent confusion in chs. 23–28. The speeches are asymmetrical in length, and one friend is missing entirely. Moreover, Job and Bildad seem to get their lines mixed up (each saying things appropriate to the other). Chapter 28 does not appear to be appropriate to either Job or one of his comforters. Do we have the original text of the dramatic poem in these chapters, or has the text been disturbed? If it has been disturbed, how should it be reconstructed?

Commentators often go beyond these 'major' source problems to question passages in YHWH's addresses and verses here and there in the dialog. All such judgments have to do with deciding on the work to be interpreted. Most critical scholars over the last century or so have assumed that we should be searching for the original dramatic poem, for it is a priceless jewel whose splendor has been partially obscured by its 'setting'.

In recent years both literary and canonical critics have challenged the 'reconstruction' of the original. It is the text in its extant, canonical form which was received by the Jewish community and adopted by the church.[18] This is the work commentators through most of history interpreted. The less one 'reconstructs', the more objective one's interpretation. Finally, close attention to the artistic patterns of the extant text will yield symmetry and meaning of a most delicate sort.[19]

This thesis of the literary and canonical critics has been charged with crypto-fundamentalism by its opponents, but in fact its view of text and communication is quite different. The typical view of fundamentalism is that the text is by one author and should be read as the 'original work'. This is the reverse side of the critical scholar who reconstructs the original work and offers an interpretation of it. The literary and canonical critics acknowledge the composite character of a text like Job, but locate the 'meaning' of the work in the final composite product rather than in the sources of which it was composed.

Can the dictum, 'interpret the text as the best text it can be', aid in the resolution of these competing views of the text to be interpreted? It can at least locate the strengths and points of vulnerability of each. Those who interpret the text as it stands obviously deserve credit for attempting to interpret the entire work. One test of a good interpretation is its comprehensiveness, its capacity to cover the entire work. Moreover, this position has the virtue of reading the same text that precritical readers had before them.

But the commitment to interpret the entire work as it stands may sacrifice coherence and elegance. The interpreter must account for the tensions, disruptions and seeming incoherences as a part of an intentional design. Interpretive history shows that this quest for unity will smooth the sharp edges and harmonize the clashing perspectives of the book. Frequently there will be recourse to what can be called 'third term' arguments,[20] the supplementation of the text with ideas which fill in the gaps. All reading requires some filling-in,[21] but we must count it an exegetical flaw to impute to a work a message which it nowhere states or implies only because a particular line of interpretation requires it for coherence.

The literary and canonical critics have a decided advantage over the single-author theory in the case of Job. The sorts of disjunctions and incoherences which are evident in the book would be counted as artistic defects if they were produced by one author, but could be counted a virtue of composite authorship.[22] We expect untidiness and unresolved disagreements in a conversation.

The strategy of reconstructing the original text of the dramatic poem and interpreting it has the virtue of coherence. The interpreter literally recreates from the textual material the best work, artistically and intellectually, the interpreter can imagine. We should expect and demand of such an interpretation a high degree of coherence, elegance and profundity.

But, of course, this strategy sacrifices comprehensiveness. To be sure, the interpreter can 'explain' everything that has been excluded from the original by reference to intrusions by editors and commentators who sought to tame the work or embellish it. But it should be admitted that such explanations are as defective as 'third term' arguments; they arise out of the interpreter's judgment as to what the dramatic poem is about.

Our dictum does not yield a clear choice between the opposing hermeneutical strategies, but it does clarify the issues. If we decide to interpret the extant text, we honor the text that it is at the expense of

coherence and elegance. If we decide to reconstruct the original
dramatic poem, we can concentrate on recreating the best text;
but this Job can be at the expense of the text that it is. It is very hard
to see how any compromise could be struck between the alternatives,
but we can be clear about the costs and benefits of each.[23]

Contextualizing the Text

A significant dimension of interpretation is the judgment as to what
texts a text should be interpreted with. What texts are 'con-texts'
with our text? We usually begin with the larger work of which the
text to be interpreted is a part. This is not a relevant consideration
regarding Job, though, for it is an independent book and in some
sense a single work.

But there are other types of context which are quite germane to
Joban interpretation. What texts are similar to Job in language, genre
and theological thinking? Can the work be located in the development
of Israelite thought? Is it a response to a specific historical situation?
Much of the history of the interpretation of this work can be
subsumed under the answers to such questions of context.

The search for the genre of the book is as productive a source of
contextualizing as one could ask for. The book is unique in
combining prose narrative and dramatic poetry, and each component
of the combination stands out within Scripture. The genre and style
of the prose prolog and epilog are distinctive within the Old
Testament,[24] but the dramatic poem is even more challenging and
significant for grasping the meaning of the book.

There are no parallels in the Old Testament to the dramatic
organization to of the work. From time to time through history
readers have compared the work to Greek tragedy and to Platonic
philosophical dialog.[25] Neither of these suggestions has been convincing,
however, for the book does not make a good tragedy or philosophical
dialog; its virtues are obscured, not illuminated, by the classification.
To be the best work Job can be, it must be given a generic
classification which befits its genius.

The search for parallels in Greek literature was probably
motivated by the absence of literature of this kind from the cultural
milieu of ancient Israel. This situation has been rectified in the last
two centuries. Among the vast quantity of texts unearthed in the
Near East, there are a number which are parallel to features of the
book of Job.[26] To cite two of the stronger ones: 'A Dialog about
Human Misery'[27] confirms the existence of the genre of the dialog

portion, namely, fictive dialog between a sufferer and a reproachful comforter; while 'Man and his God'[28] recalls Job's complaints to God about his suffering and isolation. Neither text is close enough in form and content to resolve the generic riddles of the dramatic poem as a whole, but they provide antecedents to aspects of it.

When the addresses of Job, his three companions, and YHWH are analysed into component parts, it is possible to identify parallels within the Old Testament. The book of Psalms provides the richest harvest. Most of Job's utterances are lamentation, interspersed from time to time with disputation and descriptive praise. His three companions argue with him and give counsel; YHWH's addresses are also couched in a disputational format, but they draw their content from descriptive praise. Claus Westermann, to whose formal analysis this essay is indebted, characterizes the whole book as a 'dramatized lament'.[29]

There is something of a paradox, though, in the identification of the dramatic poem as a dramatized lament. By its nature, the lament is an existential mode of speaking. One utters a lament in a time of crisis. Is an 'imaginary' lament still lamentation? Has it not been made into the vehicle for a theoretical consideration of an issue?[30] The author heightens this theoretical quality by extending Job's lamentation to include comprehensive complaints about the human condition. Combined with the argumentative exchanges with his companions, Job's lamentation could be classified as the dramatization of a skeptical position regarding the theodicy of his putative comforters. One could regard the dramatic poem as Job's debate with his friends and with God over the subject of divine justice.

And, in fact, most Biblical scholars do classify Job as wisdom. How can this classification be tested? By reflecting on the kinds of exchanges which take place between Job, his companions and YHWH in the dialog and divine revelation. Are they the sort of exchanges which make for a good airing of intellectual issues, or would they be better as some other sort of exchange?

In fact, very little in Job's addresses can be classified as arguments against a rewards and punishments theodicy, or any other intellectual question. His language is 'existential' in its complaints about his condition and the human condition in general. In the first cycle (i.e., Job 6–7, 9–10, 12–14), these complaints build toward and culminate in the form of Biblical prayer known as lament: in particular, the accusation against God, complaint about enemies, and expressions of self-pity. In the second cycle, Job loses his capacity to pray, and

expressions of hope in a reconciliation after Job's death become the dramatic highpoint of each address. Only at the end of the second cycle (chs. 21; 24) does Job address the issue of theodicy as an intellectual question. Nothing in the concluding lament (chs. 29-31) is disputational; it is all lamentation.[31]

Job's three companions do endeavor to argue in favor of a thesis regarding the causes of suffering in the first cycle. These addresses could be classified as wisdom. However, their arguments are not directed toward the establishment of a thesis, but in support of their advice to Job on how he should respond to his suffering: namely, in penitential humility. In the second cycle (chs. 15-16; 18; 20), their arguments have become implicit warnings to Job; and Eliphaz in ch. 22 directly charges Job with being godless and wicked. Thus, even in the friends' discourse argument is subordinate to existential exchanges.

Those interpreters who classify Job as wisdom do purport to find a cogent response to the problem of theodicy in YHWH's answer, but the answers found differ widely. Some find an argument for divine providence in the marvellous order of the universe.[32] Others think that Job is being taught that his suffering is of no consequence within the vast universe under divine rule.[33] Others construe the addresses as demonstrating human ignorance of the incomprehensible, mysterious ways of the Creator.[34] The more theologically inclined view the addresses as a censure of Job's pride for the '*chutzpah*' of judging YHWH; Job's concluding statements, by that account, are a genuine confession of sin.[35] Finally, a few skeptical interpreters declare YHWH's answer to be a spurious *non sequitur*.[36]

The best text dictum could be introduced to help the interpreter to decide between this strikingly discordant set of answers. Would the dramatic poem be the best work it can be with a divine *non sequitur*? Probably not; indeed, one suspects that the interpreter who takes this route believes him- or herself to be superior in intelligence and sophistication to the work. However, one might argue that the value of the dramatic poem is in raising the question, and that any answer which redeemed God's good name is spurious.

Would the work be the best work it can be if YHWH's addresses are construed as an argument for divine providence? Pious interpreters might want it to, but considered as an argument for providence, the addresses are not the most forceful argument that could be devised. The poetic transfiguration of the universe inspires a feeling of awe and sublimity, but not conviction of rational (hence, understandable)

design. The opposite view, that YHWH is showing Job that he cannot possibly understand his mysterious purposes in the universe, fits the language better. But if YHWH is demonstrating how mysterious his ways are, why should he censure Job for raising objections to his rule? If Job's ignorance is intrinsic to the human condition, he certainly is not blameworthy.

This problem is solved by the interpretation which regards Job as incurring guilt for the pride of finding fault with the ways of YHWH. This may account for the censure and repentance, but it is theologically offensive. What is wrong with standing up for one's integrity and calling the Judge of the world to account? Would the work be the best work it can be if YHWH won his case by pulling rank?

It would be even more offensive if Job were being taught that his suffering is insignificant within the economy of the universe. That would be a direct denial of the theological doctrine of *imago dei*, which by implication values each human being infinitely, i.e., worth as much as the universe as a whole.

None of the interpretations of the addresses from the whirlwind generated by the classification of Job as wisdom stand the test of our dictum very well. Even though each could be stated more elegantly and defended more earnestly, it is nevertheless doubtful that any would stand scrutiny with more than a marginally better mark.[37]

A better strategy would be to rethink the meaning of the characterization of the work as a 'dramatized lament'. What we have is a 'theoretical' representation of an existential act. What is at issue is the proper way to suffer. The author is demonstrating that the existential stance of the classical lament, with its accusations against God, constitutes 'speaking what is right' (42.7) of God, in contrast to his companions, who counsel him to accept the fact that before God humans are always in the wrong, and therefore to humble himself and throw himself on God's mercy. Job's accusations have 'legal' force,[38] and provoke a hearing of his case. YHWH's interrogation from the thunderstorm answers the cry of the supplicant and establishes justice in the trial.

Although this classification of the dramatic poem uses a modern adjective ('existential') it is congruent with much of the history of interpretation. The rabbis and church fathers assessed the dramatic poem in terms of the issue set forth in the prose prolog. These interpreters discussed whether Job continued to adhere to the ideal of piety that he exemplified in the prolog. They were uncertain, for his

language seemed to break bounds; some censured him, others made excuses.[39] They were, in our judgment, asking the right question, but their piety was too close to the friends' to give the best answer. They could not entertain the possibility that a person might enact righteousness and faithfulness in this protesting, accusing fashion.

Some modern critics have come closer to seeing the dramatic poem as Job's quest for a hearing from God.[40] They understand that the issue of theodicy is dramatically embodied in the person of Job, and are willing to justify Job's questioning. Unfortunately, the insight is somewhat lost by the construal of YHWH's addresses as censure for Job's questioning, a censure to which Job capitulates. This leaves the work divided against itself, justifying Job's protests and then condemning them.

For Job to be the best work it can be, YHWH's addresses should affirm his right to protest and find fault with his rule of the world, yet convince Job that YHWH is worthy of praise for his just and merciful deeds. It could be argued, for example, that the fact that YHWH speaks is as important as what he says.[41] As to what he says, it should be an answer to the cry of the supplicant.[42] The tone of censure does not necessarily imply divine judgment upon what Job has said; it could be the language of insistent challenge to accept his status as a creature. Job's responses can be translated and construed as congruent with this understanding of the divine addresses.[43]

Note that the generic question has led to the question of content, to the question of what Job is about. To assess the value of various generic classifications, one has to work through every facet of the dramatic poem. It was argued that the wisdom classification did not really fit either the dialog or YHWH's addresses, and that a more 'existential' issue, namely, how to pray in the midst of arbitrary suffering, makes better sense of this 'dramatized lament'.[44] The issue of theodicy is obviously present, but it is embedded in the existential issue and resolved in personal, dramatic terms.

The Particular, Unique Text
A text is not only an instance of a genre, but a particular and potentially unique configuration of language.[45] The search for its genre begins to define its uniqueness, but one must go further. We need to understand what it is communicating to its audience and how it establishes and manages the communicative relationship. This includes the whole range of its rhetorical devices and structures,

but goes beyond them to the character it projects, and the transaction it engenders with its audience.

One of the questions that arises particularly with the book of Job has to do with sequence. Reading a work involves grasping how the incidents follow one another. In Job there are some abrupt changes not only in genre, but also in perspective (between chs.2 and 3, and again between 42.6 and 42.7-17). Within the dialog, the style of dramatization leaves some question of whether the reading sequence is meant to be progressing toward a dramatic resolution or not. Finally, the exchanges between YHWH and Job at the end of the poetic drama (38.1-42.6) are mysteriously ambiguous; as we shall see this exchange is very important to the rhetoric of the book.

Let us begin with the relationship of the prose prolog and epilog to the dramatic poem. As readers, we are confronted with an abrupt change from narrative to drama, then from drama back to narrative. Not only is this a generic change, the perspective changes just as sharply. The Job of the prolog and epilog is a paragon of conventional piety. The God of the prose narrative is the patriarch of a pantheon who is willing to suspend justice to demonstrate a point to a skeptical member of the divine court. When the test is over, and Job has vindicated God's claims, Job is restored and compensated for his troubles. The poetic drama contrasts at every point. Job no longer exhibits the masochistic piety of the prolog. God is the sole sovereign power of existence who, for that very reason, is a potential tyrant. The world portrayed is more 'realistic' and the theology more profound.

What interpretation of the relationship of the two parts of the work makes it the best work it can be? Should the contrasts be harmonized or accentuated? Is the meaning of the work to be found in continuity or juxtaposition? If in juxtaposition, how does each part comment on and qualify the other? What aspects of the narrative are to be carried over to the drama, and what are to be set aside as no longer operative? What purpose does the 'polytheism' of the prolog serve in the work?

The best interpretation of Job would construe each part in its best light, and see them as enhancing each other. The prolog paints the scene in virtually parabolic colors.[46] Not only does it recount the course of events that descended on Job, it establishes his identity as a righteous and pious man. Is this identity to be imputed to the Job of the dramatic poem? One either has to regard him as falling away from his virtue, or enacting it in a new, more controversial way. The

latter is the better line of interpretation, for the dramatic poem arouses our identification with him and his cause.[47] The semi-polytheistic theology of the prolog can be construed as simple 'folk piety', or as the theology appropriate to a Gentile. The latter would be artistically and theologically more interesting. The shift to radical monotheism in the drama dissolves the external point of view of the prolog, collapsing the horizons of story and Biblical reader. The epilog then distances the reader again, allowing us to relax after the grueling ordeal of the dramatic poem.

Another kind of problem of sequence confronts the reader in the dramatic poem. The early critic, Robert Lowth, raised it nicely in one of his lectures on Job in *De Sacra Poesi Habaeorum* (1753).[48] He admitted that the poem is dramatic in the trivial sense, but argued that it lacks some necessary features of classical drama. According to Aristotle, whose *Poetics* he was following, a drama is the representation of an action; the plot of the action must not only be a unity; it must at least involve some 'perplexity or embarrassment' which is resolved by a series of connected events.[49] By such a definition, Job is not a drama, for it

> contains no plot or action whatsoever. . .: it uniformly exhibits one constant state of things, not the smallest change of fortune taking place from the beginning to the end; and it contains merely a representation of those manners, passions, and sentiments that might be expected in such a situation.[50]

He does not even allow that God's addresses and Job's change of heart represent a 'change of fortune'.[51]

There are two related issues here. Do dramatic changes have to be 'changes of fortune', or do changes in relationships, character and deportment also deserve this appellation? If the latter, do such changes occur as a course of connected events in the book of Job?

Behind these questions, one has to ask whether it makes any difference. Would the dramatic poem be a better work if there is an action unfolding and being resolved than if there were not? Lowth gives a weak 'no',[52] assuring the reader that it is 'in its kind most beautiful and perfect'. However, there are sound reasons for affirming the contrary. If the dialog can be read as an unfolding action, we can interpret later utterances as responses to earlier ones, and understand earlier utterances as having consequences; we can observe relationships and character undergo changes, and we can construe the intervention of God as an organic resolution of the

conflict of the dialog. Thus, the meaning of the poem is enriched greatly by regarding it as a plotted action.

Of course, an interpreter of Lowth's persuasion might object that we are essentially expressing a preference for a different work than what lies before us. He or she would have to grant that changes in relationships, character and deportment count as action, but would deny that such changes occur in Job. The issue comes down to this: Do the addresses of Job and his companions in the dialog read better as a static expression of 'manners, passions and sentiments' appropriate to the situation or as an unfolding of an action tending toward a denouement? Do they constitute a second rate—at best— dramatic development but a first rate representation of unchanging conditions and attitudes?

Complicating the issue is the decision as to the lineaments of the work we are interpreting. Chapters 24–28 do not fit the dramatic sequence observable in chs. 3–23. Up to ch. 24, we can observe the friends change from counselling Job to warning him to witnessing (falsely) against his character (ch. 22).[53] Job works up the courage to confront God with challenges to his judgment (ch. 13), then loses the capacity to pray and begins to hope for a reconciliation after his death (chs. 17; 19).[54] After Eliphaz's accusations against Job in ch. 22, the dialog should be over; Job should turn his back on his comforters and hope against hope that God will rectify the situation.[55] The material in chs. 24–28 obscures this resolution, and the standard reconstruction of the third cycle actually aggravates it.[56] So we are left with the problem with which we began: What work are we interpreting?

Do the addresses of YHWH from the whirlwind resolve the action of the dialog?[57] What would we have to find in them to confirm that they do? How would one interpret them to make them the most fitting resolution of the dialog?

We have already discussed the generic aspect of this question. Obviously the addresses would have to be a fitting answer to the question or issue of the dialog. In addition, though, the addresses would have to be dramatically appropriate to the situation that has been depicted in the dialog and to the expectations the work has aroused in the audience.

The work would be better if the divine intervention were not arbitrary—something on the order of a *deus ex machina*—but the fulfillment of the preceding action. Obviously, Job has been hoping for and provoking such a theophany. The world depicted in the

dialog involved a God acting everywhere, and communicating his will through various means. So, the theophany itself does not shatter the dramatic logic already established. It would, however, be a case of *deus ex machina* if YHWH introduced new knowledge—knowledge to which the deity alone is privy. For the work to be the best work of art, the divine addresses should draw upon knowledge already acknowledged by the participants. The reader would, thereby, be able to experience the outcome as a resolution, not an imposition.

The reader has been encouraged to identify with Job and reject the viewpoint of his comforters. If one happens to agree with the position of the comforters, one will be irritated by the outcome of the dialog. Elihu speaks for such a reader: '[He] was angry—angry at Job because he thought himself right against God. He was angry as well at his three friends because they found no reply, but merely condemned Job' (32.2-3). The divine addresses must confirm Job's stance or convince the reader that he deserved to be censured and forced to repent. Elihu desires the latter, but the reader may well have been won over to Job's side and be offended by any violation of his integrity.

The prose prolog has already posited that Job has no skeletons in the closet that YHWH could drag out to convict him. If Job has done anything to arouse the divine wrath, we have witnessed it. Elihu condemns him for justifying himself rather than God. Although one may quibble over the best characterization of Job's action, this is a fairly accurate way of describing what he has done. The question is whether he was right to do so. Was his suffering arbitrary? Was the guilt implied by such suffering a righteous judgment? Does a pious person have to accept whatever God metes out, even when he seems to be a hostile foe or tyrannical judge?

Some aspects of YHWH's answer seem to confirm Elihu's attitude; other aspects to confirm the righteousness and truthfulness of Job. Only the righteous receive a hearing from God (13.16); Job receives a hearing. Moreover, God does not have to attain a name for justice at the expense of human innocence (40.8). The questions YHWH puts to Job aim not to degrade him, but to elicit his praise of his Creator and Lord. On the other hand, YHWH does not show sympathy for Job, or acknowledge the truth of his complaints, or offer any explanation. Rather, the tone is impersonal, censorious, and perhaps sarcastic. Elihu too can find confirmation of his interpretation.

Job's final response (42.2-6) does not resolve opposing interpretations, for it can be translated to conform to a number of alternatives.[58] Recently it has been argued that the language of this response is

deliberately ambiguous. 'The author used language in such a way as to allow the reader's understanding of Yahweh's revelation to interpret Job's response'.[59] This was a conscious artistic strategy:

> (T)he poet himself intended no explicit resolution to the tension that exists in the Yahweh speech(es) between the very fact of Yahweh's presence and the actual contents of the divine address. Rather, he created a situation that can be interpreted in several ways according to the theological inclinations of the reader.[60]

This understanding of the resolution of Job is quite compelling, and generates a number of further insights into the work.

While one could construe the ambiguous ending as evidence that the author could not resolve the issue that he posed, or lacked the courage to present it to an unreceptive community, it should be appreciated—in the light of the aesthetic hypothesis—as a sophisticated rhetorical move. Rather than allow the reader to stand back and pass judgment on the adequacy of the resolution, the author forces us to complete the meaning of the work. The resolution has the parabolic quality of involving the audience in the action.[61]

Note that the ambiguity is circumscribed. The work is sufficiently structured to eliminate all but a few avenues of resolution.[62] All center on YHWH's revelation; the reader is forced to consider how Job—and by implication, the reader—should respond to divine revelation. All solutions are theocentric; there is no room here for religious agnosticism.

The ambiguity evokes the mystery of life with God. The reader is forced to admit that the reality of God does not dispel the mystery of existence, but heightens it. We cannot be certain about any scheme of interpretation, for we are aware that there are cogent alternatives. One might say that we are forced to admit that God will be God, and not the predictable guarantor of anyone's scheme of coherence.

Nevertheless, the ambiguous resolution entices us to work out our understanding. Rather than shrugging our shoulders in despair of unravelling the ambiguity, we do in fact take up the task of completing the work. The appearance of YHWH instills a sense of urgency; God is too real and pressing to ignore. Job's compact, cryptic utterances hint at a profound change in his soul, a 'shaking of the foundations' of mystic proportions.[63] We are drawn into the struggle to understand what that change consists of, for it promises to unlock the door to our salvation.

Our dictum that we interpret Job as the best work it can be should

guide us in our struggle. Obviously Job's answer must be organically related to the entire dramatic poem and indirectly to the prose prolog and epilog. We are forced back into a consideration of the action of Job, his companions, and YHWH. If the central issue of the dialog is existential, and YHWH's addresses are an answer to Job's lament, Job's final utterance must be an expression of the integrity which animated his quest. We readers could not join Job in his reconciliation with YHWH if we were not convinced of YHWH's worthiness. A God who overwhelmed Job by his deity, rather than convincing him of his worthiness, would not elicit our respect. If Job does repent, we must be convinced that he has spoken in illicit pride—either of knowledge or of righteousness. If we reject the God who speaks from the whirlwind, we must reject the One who has convinced Job, a man of integrity, of his worthiness.

Chapter 6

GENESIS AND POWER:
AN ANALYSIS OF THE BIBLICAL STORY OF CREATION[1]

The relationship between truth and power has fascinated philosophers and rhetoricians for centuries. The basic problematic of the relationship may be traced to the truism that truth-claims are made through discourse, and, as such, must be made persuasively. Therefore, the will to truth would seem to be subverted by the will to power. On the other hand, in those areas that matter to us and in which we consider ourselves to be expert, we assume we can somehow break out of whatever persuasive power the discourse holds over us, compare it with something else, and thus assess its truth or falsity. Such has been the starting point of academic theories of knowledge in all their manifold forms; they claim to produce 'truths' because the will to power can be transcended by the will to truth, if the will to truth is properly enacted.

It is perhaps a desire to undermine the claims of objective truth obtained through the disinterested application of the proper method that has led some thinkers in the twentieth century to want to develop a discourse-centered theory of power—to discover that quality of discourse which gives the discourse sufficient power to determine what people will take to be truth.[2] We are in sympathy with this theoretical direction, but believe it may be easier to clarify the relationship between discourse and power by analyzing a clear example of discourse that has had and continues to have a presumption not just that it represents truth, but that it is truth. Such a presumption have been associated with the central narratives of the Hebrew Bible.

It seems that narrative, more than the other types of discourse appearing in the Bible, embodies that 'form of life' in which people are most likely to find truth. As Alasdair MacIntyre has observed,

'He [the human being] is not essentially, but becomes through his history, a teller of stories that aspire to truth. I can only answer the question of what am I to do if I can answer the prior question, of what story do I find myself a part'.[3] What we take for truth and what we respond to as powerful appears to be a feature of narrative structure.[4] Thus we believe that an analysis of Biblical narrative will reveal the peculiar quality of discourse that makes it seem powerful enough to establish the conditions of knowledge.

With few exceptions to date, those who have attempted a discourse-centered theory of power have approached discourse from an aesthetic perspective.[5] Those investigating narrative in contemporary Biblical studies have likewise approached narrative primarily against the background of literature and poetics.[6] Such terms as 'art', 'beauty', and 'timeless truths' come to mind as associated with this enterprise. Literary or poetic concerns, in other words, incline us to see narrative structures as if they were involved primarily with the will to truth rather than the will to power, as competitors with positivism seeking after the same goal, different only by measure of method and attitude. Thus Biblical critics have sought to understand the power of the text by establishing its aesthetic truth, its historical truth, or in extreme cases, its status as ultimate religious truth. While different aspects of the text's character have been illuminated by these approaches, its power has remained beyond their grasp.

But there is another route to follow, the route of Isocrates and Cicero, where the focus is still on narrative, but narrative considered primarily as rhetoric rather than poetry. The words of the Bible were meant to persuade its audience to right action, or what the Biblical authors considered to be right action, and so it is the success of the text as persuasive discourse which is most likely to account for the power of these words to endure through time.[7] There were many good stories, detailed histories, and forceful testimonies that did not survive. The Bible assumes the narrative shape that it does, not because it is most beautiful or most truthful, but rather because this is the form that is most persuasive. The whole tone of the Bible is what Northrop Frye calls 'concerned address'.[8] Such discourse finds its end not in what its words are, but in what they do to and for an audience. If our object is a theory of power, it would seem better to think of the narratives which contain it as rhetoric, intimately and primarily concerned with the will to power.

The will to power is perhaps most evident in Genesis 1–3. Faced with the apparent addition of this primeval history to the already

existing sacred history beginning with ch.12, commentators have perennially asked why the Bible does not simply begin with the received sacred traditions recounting YHWH's choosing of Israel as his people and the making of the covenant.[9] This sacred history presumes YHWH's power in the world, but does not account for it. Genesis 1–3 prefaces this history with an account of his power that is forceful enough to sustain the story of YHWH's miraculous interventions which follow. The power of Genesis 1–3 is great enough to have enabled the story of creation it contains to endure to this day even after the onslaught of scientific evidence which contradicts its details. Genesis 1–3 is also powerful enough to have established the sacredness of the discourse it introduces. Thus, we have chosen Genesis 1–3 as the textual focus of our study not only because it is about power, but also because the discourse itself is powerful enough to establish the conditions of sacred knowledge.

The Text

Analysis of Genesis 1–3 is complicated, of course, by the fact that it is not one text but two. This division of the text into its original separate documents has presented Biblical scholars with a dilemma. Even though the text might have been originally composed as separate accounts of creation, it has been read by both the traditional Jewish and Christian communities as an integrated whole. How, then, can one be faithful to both the integrity of the separate documents discovered by Biblical scholarship and the integrity of the whole as intended by the final redactor and as read by the intended audiences?

We decided to deal with this dilemma by a 'best text' reading, which first examines J and P as each reads independently of the other, and then, based on the meanings obtained from each individually, reads them together as a single narrative. Our examination of P and J together also takes account of the fact that P was composed later, but then placed before J in the text. This would seem to indicate that P is meant to comment upon or interpret J in some superordinate way to subsequent readers. Our reading of P thus attempts to discover and transcribe this commentary as well.

The differences between P and J in both form and content are, of course, covered well by Biblical scholars.[10] Our approach to reading the two texts both separately and as one, however, yielded a distinctive view of the relationship between P and J, especially

against the background of a search for a discourse-centered theory of power. We shall argue that each text contains both a different view of God's power in the world and a distinctive way of representing that power to a human audience as 'truth'. When read separately, each text, as an account of the power of God and an example of the power of discourse, is incomplete. But each is permitted to realize fully the part of the picture it represents because each is complemented by the other. We will show that together the texts of Genesis 1–3 contain a full-bodied, balanced, and persuasive expression of a complete vision of power.

This exegetical exercise will also serve to exemplify how the 'best text' approach might be applied to a text which presents possibilities for meaning both in its separate constituent documents as well as in the final redaction passed down by the tradition. We now proceed to our examination of each text separately in the chronological order of their composition, beginning with J, or the Yahwist.

'*J*'

The primary interest of the Yahwist account is not really in the origins of the universe or even in human origins *per se*, but rather in the origins of the human condition: How did human beings come to their present predicament in relationship to God? Thus, unlike his colleague in ch. 1, J dispenses with the details of creation rather perfunctorily (2.4b-7). He expends little effort in establishing the precise sequence of creation and is unconcerned about the amount of time involved. For J, God's power is best understood not by standing in awe before the 'facts' of creation, but by a sensitive narrative comprehension of how God's relationship to humankind is constructed. Consequently, rather than dwelling on the details of how the world was created, the Yahwist's story of 'creation' emphasizes the important elements which set the scene for the crucial conflict in the Garden which follows. These elements are the creation of man and woman, the simple joys of life in the Garden before the eating of the fruit, and, of course, the prohibition against eating of the 'Tree of Knowledge'. Each of these elements is narrated in a way which heightens the dramatic intensity and gives us insight into the relationships among the characters. The burden of J's account of creation, which takes up the rest of ch. 2 and all of ch. 3, builds upon these dramatic elements to tell the story of Eve's temptation by the serpent, her enticing Adam to share the forbidden fruit, God's

confronting Adam and Eve with their mistake, and finally their expulsion from the Garden.

To appreciate fully the rhetorical choices made by J to lend power to his account, let us first examine the possibilities the author rejected. His account clearly is not an *encomium* to the glory of divine creation. Unlike P, J does not bring power to his story by means of an awe-inspiring description of how order was created out of chaos. He also does not make any substantial use of the ancient mythic formulas from other traditions which would have resonated authoritatively for his Mesopotamian-bred audience.[11] He chooses to begin his story outside the bounds of the ancient core of sacred history that we find repeated in numerous places throughout the Pentateuch.[12] In short, J's story seems rhetorically conceived deliberately to avoid drawing power from sources outside itself.

Instead, J chooses to compose, almost *de nova*, a very human 'pastoral'. Rather than a divine presence controlling the forces of creation from above, God enters the scene as a very human character. The story itself unfolds not as a pure expression of divine will ('Let there be light... and it was so' [Gen. 1.3]), but as a description of the actions and interactions of the characters in the story. J, as narrator, appears to bargain in good faith with his characters, letting them dictate the flow of the story, rather than declaring his message through a series of pronouncements about God. It seems that J chooses to depend entirely on the story he has to tell to give his message whatever power it will have. Thus J's text provides us with an extraordinary experiment in the use of the narrative form to lend power to sacred knowledge.

The power of a sacred text is such that it enables the text to reach beyond the temporal limitations of the author, and effectively communicate its message to audiences far removed from the author in time and space.[13] While the original author may lay claim, implicitly or explicitly, to divine revelation as the source of his authority, once written down, the knowledge contained in a sacred text can no longer be revealed oracularly to succeeding generations. Cast into a narrative form like J's, a sacred text depends primarily on the universal appeal of its characters: Adam must indeed be 'everyman' and YHWH everyman's God. J's appropriation of the narrative form also requires that his ideas about human beings and God be conveyed through the deeds and experiences of his characters, rather than simply pronounced '*ex cathedra*'.

Adam's creation from an amalgam of divine breath and earthly

matter is a narrative reflection of the ambiguities of human nature. The earthly matter represents the limits of our bodies, and the divine breath, the seemingly infinite possibilities of our minds and its fantasies of what could be. The Tree of Knowledge of Good and Evil and the prohibition against eating its fruit express the implications of this ambiguity. The world contains what appear to be the material agents, that, if used effectively, would enable us to realize our grandiose fantasies of being like gods, but, at the same time, also contain the seeds of our inevitable destruction.

The deity of the story is highly anthropomorphized. From the very start, he is more of this world than a higher one. The verbs used to describe his creative work are descriptive of an earthly craftsman: God 'forms', 'fashions', and 'plants', and the material he works with is all of this earth. Most of his action is in fact reaction to what man and woman do. He does not so much create a world and determine its course as he sets a scene and responds to the other actors within the bounds of that scene. He is, like J, a narrator, waiting to see what his characters will do to see how the story will turn out. The 'sources of action' in the story are as many as the characters present in the scene, and the course of the story hinges upon the exercise of free will within the limits and possibilities of each character's nature.

The Yahwist's representation of God's power is not an abstract presentation of propositions that would depend on the particular biases of a cultural situation for their authority, but rather is expressed through the universally appealing concreteness of an archetypal confrontation between humans and God. The scene in the Garden between God and human beings after the eating of the fruit epitomizes this communication of theology through the dynamics of the narrative form. The scene is a pastoral evocation of a father discovering his child with his hands in the proverbial cookie jar. God's calling to Adam, 'Where are you?' (3.9) might be more accurately rendered in this context as 'And what have you been up to just now?'[14] As the archetypal child, Adam, of course, first tries to shift the blame. God's response is sure and swift punishment, but with a father's solicitude for his children's physical and psychic well-being (3.21).

This is not the awesome God, creator of heaven and earth, but God as stern but loving father to the man-child Adam and woman-child Eve, and by narrative implication to the audience as well. As the narrative progressively reveals the father–child relationship, the audience is invited to experience itself in the same relationship to

God through identification with the very real and universal characters. As the story takes Adam and Eve from the innocence of childhood to the hard realities of adulthood, the audience is led from its reminiscence of a childlike relationship to God as father to a new understanding of its separation from God and its urge to return. The story speaks not of God as an independent divine entity, but God as the audience might experience him in the story of its own life. God's power has no existence outside of his interaction with the human beings in the story. His power is disclosed to the audience through the audience's own identification with the human characters and the appeal of God's character in the story as father.

The narrative is thus not an argumentative imposition upon the audience's thinking, but a transaction with its experience. Its 'truth' depends on its capacity to evoke the isomorphic meanings in human experience as lived by the characters in the story and as lived by the audience. Its attempt at this evocative truth is transparent. The narrator has nothing to hide behind. If this is not the way life is, that fact will be readily apparent to the audience. J tells us not only that he sees the relationship of humans to God as a father–child relationship, but he also shows us how he came to conceive of the relationship in this way and how he would have us conceive of it. The narrator tries to tell the story as truly as he can, but the process of his trying is there for the audience to see and assess. The audience might say the telling does not ring true, and the narrator must accept that judgment, for all his claims to authority are there in the telling. He holds nothing over his audience save the power that the story might have over both of them; thus J permits his authority to remain potential, waiting upon his audience's response to the unfolding of the characters and the events of his story.

The Yahwist's narrative contract with the audience also involves telling only about that which both the author and the audience might know. He does not move beyond the transaction and elevate himself above his audience by dwelling on his personal knowledge of the deity and the deeds of the deity that lie beyond the audience's understanding. Nothing of what God does in the story subsequent to the actual creation is peculiarly divine. They are the actions of any parent in a similar situation, though the range of God's 'parenting' permits his judgments to take place on a much wider scale.

Thus J's narratological inquiry into the relationship between human beings and God is conducted through a story that is firmly grounded in the material and social world in which the author and

audience both live. He brings his thoughts about God down to a level where they can be subjected to the judgment of his audience. His anthropomorphisms make God accessible to human knowing. God's relationship to human beings unfolds in a story which can be about every person who reads it, and every person who reads it can judge for himself the truth of the telling and the truth of the actions being told. J, therefore, solves the problem of making his text powerful by his skillful appropriation of the narrative form.

The Yahwist's use of the narrative form to give his discourse power is intimately bound up with his vision of YHWH's power. As the power of the text is a function of the transaction between the experience of the characters in the story and the experience of the audience, so the power of YHWH grows out of a transaction of wills in conflict with one another. God does not impose his power on his human creations, but rather lets it emerge out of the conflict between his character and the aspirations and limitations of human nature.

God creates Adam, but part of the creation is the very intimate sharing of breath with him. God then invites Adam to participate in the completion of creation as a kind of partner by naming the animals which God makes, tilling the Garden which God plants, and even having woman built with a part of himself, as God gave a part of himself to the creation of man. The seeming invitation to partnership in creation suggests an ambiguity in God's power. The ambiguity continues to manifest itself as God completely leaves the stage, and Man and Woman are left to act on their own. Without God's continued presence, the limits he sets seem surmountable. It appears to be very much the human's Garden—the possibilities, without limit.

The relationship between God and human beings as we know it is an outgrowth of a transaction—a transaction that follows in elegant narrative logic from the ambiguities in God's power and the response of human nature to those ambiguities. Human beings want the power of the godhead: to know good and evil and to be full partners in the creation of the world. But their knowledge is not to be as powerful as God's. God punishes them by 'uncreating', by diminishing the partnership as originally conceived and by distancing humans from himself and the creative process. Human beings will have to work and bear great pain to keep themselves alive and to procreate. Outside the garden, they will also have to decide continually between good and evil. Before eating of the forbidden fruit, their intimate partnership with God made those decisions unnecessary. Once they

tried to become more like God through gaining knowledge of good and evil, they were burdened with the indeterminate moral quality of their actions. They would never know for sure if their actions were good or evil in God's eyes. They would need God's law to guide their actions, but they could never be certain of how God might judge those actions.

The certainty the Yahwist expresses about God's power is that it follows the logic of a story that rings true. But this certainty is crucial given the insecurity engendered by God's seemingly arbitrary choice of Israel described later in the sacred history and the implicit possibility of an equally arbitrary rejection. J's preface asserts that this awesome power to choose and reject follows a story line that carries with it a predictable course. God's expulsion of Adam and Eve from the Garden was not a premeditated act, but a response to Adam and Eve's disobedience of God's cardinal rule. God participated in the story that Man and Woman helped create by their own actions. The prophets would later pick up this theme and apply the same narrative logic both to explain what happened to Israel and to predict what would happen. Man and Woman were thus co-creators of their own destiny. We call this vision of power 'authority'.[15] It arises out of the give and take of divine and human action, each conceived as having reciprocal force. It results from the conflict and negotiation of wills rather than being imposed unilaterally from above.

The Yahwist asserts, contrary to the Hebrew prophets, that God's ways are in fact our ways.[16] His power is not inexplicable wilfulness, but a transaction framed by narrative logic. The outrageous forces loose in the universe funnel down to us in an ordered form through the narrative contract between God and human beings. J's story is a persuasive rendition of how that contract is realized in our world.

'P'

Genesis 1.1–2.4a is a dignified liturgy which depicts the seven days of creation in a manner that seems deliberately measured and balanced. Each day is filled with a discrete and unique activity, contributing to the fullness of creation. Each of these acts is introduced and concluded in a starkly styled phrase which, through repetition, becomes a motif: 'And God said, "Let there be"', 'and it was so', 'and God saw that it was good', 'and there was evening and there was morning, a. . . day'. In its worst light, the Priestly Writer's phrasing could be thought impersonal and ingenuously studied; but in its best light, such language can be perceived as a stately, grand, decorously

underplayed portrayal of an an almost unimaginable act of will, the act of creating a universe.

Stylistically, P confines himself to a series of claims about God's activity in the world. The argumentative space around the claims is not filled in with the accouterments of the narrative form. The claims simply stand, without the support of surrounding story. By confining himself to claims about divine activity with which the audience has no experience, the author essentially demands assent from the audience rather than appealing to its experience for corroboration, as does J. The audience's participation in this form of sacred discourse is minimal. The audience either accepts the claims made by the author or rejects them at its peril.

Where the Yahwist achieved the power of sacredness by creating intimacy with the audience through the universal appeal of his characters, the Priestly Writer imbues his text with power by creating distance from the audience. He speaks to his auditors from on high, overpowering them with his knowledge of the mysteries of divine creation—knowledge which to them is unfathomable. His vision of God's power predisposes him to eschew the intimacy and parity with the audience of literary narrative.

There are at least four important impressions attendant upon the content of P's account: (1) It is crucial that God speaks directly; God always appears as the subject of P's sentences, a cosmic organizer who in his speaking exercises full control over primordial chaos. He creates through the active power of his word, determining in the speech act itself that the word spoken will become the word fulfilled.

(2) Further, unlike the polytheistic creation myths in Mesopotamia, P presents creation as the work of one deity who has no female consort and needs not battle other supernatural wills.[17] Sun, moon, and stars were independent deities in Babylonian tradition, but in Gen. 1.16-18 they are divested of divinity and made vassals responsible to one sovereign deity.

(3) Additionally, the Priestly Writer recognizes the innate excellence of creation and celebrates it in the frequent formal refrain, 'And God saw that it was good', and in the climax reached in v. 31, 'And behold, it was very good'. No asceticism is fostered here. Rather, P proposes that before human beings praised Elohim for the wondrous work of creation, the deity contemplated his own creative work and delighted in its integrity and inherent beauty.

(4) Moreover, P seems to build an irony into his description of the relationship between God and human beings. At first, one is impressed with the dignity and power of humanity's place in God's creation: Made in the divine image, human beings are God's representatives on earth who will govern the plant and animal environment. Yet, on closer study, one notes that human beings are never the subject of a P sentence; they are confined always to grammatical objectivity. So there is the distance between God and humanity that exists between active subject and passive object: Human existence and sovereignty derive solely from Elohim.

From a purely literary or dramatistic perspective, it seems difficult to think of the Priestly account of creation as a narrative. There is but one character who acts—without motive or passion or self-fulfiling purposes in a scene specifically described as a void and formless waste of water and darkness. The created world is a scene for the realization of creaturely potential, not divine; God superintends but does not participate or 'live in' his own creation. He is of the Heavens and not of this world, so we know only what he does, never what he is, or what motivates him. There is no conflict in creation and no question regarding the capacity of God to create something from nothing.

The only mark of literary or dramatistic narrative is the structure of P's account: Action is divided into seven parts, and each of the parts is related in such a way as to mark the passage of time, suggesting that creation was a staged or planned process.

From a rhetorical perspective, however, the Priestly account is a narrative by measure of its *function*. In rhetoric, *narratio* is not a *form* of discourse, but a *feature* of discourse—that part of the written or spoken oration which describes and limits the reader's or audience member's field of action.[18] In courts of law, for example, a juror must hear the defendant's 'story' as told by defense counsel and by the prosecutor before judgment as to innocence or guilt is possible: That which the contending parties will argue about is established early on as the 'story of the crime'. It is, from this perspective, impossible for a 'narrative' to 'stand alone' as it may in literature or drama. All rhetorical narratives necessarily require interpretation and are incomplete until arguments and proofs are marshalled to advise readers and audience members what it is they must do or believe as a result of the story they have heard. If there appears to be a naked narrative, we should understand that arguments, proofs, and actions

are implicit, for narratives either recommend and promote or condemn and repress the action they portray.

If Biblical scholars are correct in their inference that the Priestly Writer's *narratio* was attached as a prologue to the older Yahwist account, it is important to realize that P stood in relationship to an inherited text as critic and interpreter, in precisely the same relationship we now stand. J was a part of P's world, something to contemplate, a story with a moral to discover and appreciate.

The Priestly Writer, however, did not merely criticize as a result of his contemplation of J; he tampered with a sacred text. Now he did not, so far as we know, take his blue pencil to J, changing this word and that phrase to suit his felt need; but he did *add* to J, attaching *narratio* to narrative as one would add an adjective to a noun. Why? Among those who see differences in the Genesis account of creation, there has never been a doubt that, at least in comparison with J, P's contribution to the Torah is rhetorical; indeed, the very designation 'Priestly account' is, as we have already remarked, an indication that P's writing seems to communicate the attitudes of a theocracy. Simply conceiving that P writes from the viewpoint and to the advantage of a priestly class establishes that the account is rhetorical.

But there seems more to learn from understanding that P's operations are the same as an advocate's: What impression of J did P want us to develop? Why would P want to alter our perception of the tradition itself rather than simply criticize or comment upon an unchanging, immutable text?

If P's account is rhetorically a *narratio*, its adjectival appendage to J seems to recommend that we read J as an argument and an interpretation, a series of proofs which illuminate or amplify P's stating of the case—P's story, not of a crime, but of the act of creation. P evidently conceived that there was a lack in J of a frame of reference, and that feeling was so strong that it justified tampering with the sacred. Now we have already tried a preliminary interpretation of J, and we will in the next section interpret P and J together, but it seems useful here to read P alone, seeing J, anticipating J, through the terms and resources of P's rhetoric. If we had not read J and knew only that P was establishing a frame of reference for J, what can we learn about what P thought lacking in J? Reviewing our preliminary impressions of P's *narratio* should provide some answers:

1. God speaks directly, is always the subject of P's sentences, and creates through the active power of his word. The power portrayed

seems quite literally authorial, the same power over all of life that writers enjoy over their sentences. As we may choose one word and not another, rub one out, or rip up the sheet on which we write, so God simply chooses things, rubs them out, rips them up, and so has an absolute power. J, in other words, must in P's mind be read in the frame of realizing that God is the author of the universe and is thus not only *above* all other powers, but *prior* to them: P tried mightily to communicate the idea of *nothing*, and from nothing *something*, portraying the awesome intervening force that made the difference. P's *narratio* leaves J enough argumentative or interpretive space to be read equivocally, now *presuming* God's authorial power, now *proving* such power, now exploring the consequences of such power in interaction with human will.

2. Unlike other deities in other religious systems, God is *alone* in the scene of creation. This portrayal qualifies authorial power in an important way: This essay, for example, is a collaboration. As these words were written, one of us had an apparent authorial power to choose this or that word and to rub out what seemed wrong or inappropriate. When we came together, however, each of us had to negotiate to keep a pet sentence or to strike another's phrase that grated on the ear. God did not have to negotiate in the act of creation, according to P; he worked alone, with no other creature of force to say him nay. So whatever J says must be read in the frame of realizing that there is no appeal from authorial power save to the author himself—God, and only God, can alter the words that have been written.

3. What God created is *intrinsically* good: In P's account, God does not *infer* that his creation is good, nor does he search for confirmation of the quality of his creation; rather, God *sees* that it is good, *says* that it is good, and that settles it. What can be seen and proclaimed must be self-evident. Now goodness is a quality, not an object—none of us has ever seen a 'good' walking down the street. But God *sees* goodness; even as a quality it is self-evident in his eyes. Whatever J says, in other words, should be read in the context of knowing that authorial power like God's extends even to evaluations of creation. Unlike writers or actors, God needs no favorable review or applause, for his art is so perfect that it contains its own self-evident goodness.

4. God exalts human beings in P's frame, but he keeps them always in the objective case. Humans matter, but not because they

are individual subjects, capable of being actors on the stage God occupies. Like actors performing the script of a playwright, men and women can only act out what has been written, 'strutting and fretting their brief hour upon the stage'. If there is villainy or heroism, accomplishment or failure, P wants it understood that the author is ultimately responsible, not the actors; humanity is as significant as a playing piece at chess. In P's mind, whatever J says should be read in the frame of realizing that freedom of will in human beings exists only as the actor's craft in relation to an author's script. Human will, in other words, is a matter of style, nuance, balance, and emphasis, not a matter of creativity or authorship.

In sum, the Priestly Writer seems to have decided that the lack in the Yahwist's account was an understanding of the nature of divine power, specifically the power of authorship. Each important feature of P's narrative describes or qualifies the kind of power writers and speakers have over the choice of word, phrase, content, and outcome of what is written or spoken. With regard to the nature of authorial power, P asserts that God-as-author possessed an absolutely unqualified capacity to create, constrained neither by the task of creation nor by need to take other similar powers into account.

With regard to the consequences of authorial power, P wants it understood that products of creation are intrinsically good no matter what opinion an audience or critic might have. Further, he wants it understood that authorial power extends even into the arena of human will, restricting a most favored creation to the status of objects able to initiate action only as nuance or emphasis. If P's *narratio* is an adjectival appendage to J's narration, we may infer that the concept of divine power J presupposes is incomplete, or easily misunderstood, without a frame of reference to establish what the power of authorship consists of. It remains for us to describe P and J together, as a whole, to see what *power* of a piece may be, what adjective and noun mean as a unity of expression.

'P–J'

The human need that correlates with the authorial dimension of power would seem to be the need for certainty: to know what is right and to do what is right. P responds to this need with the directness it requires in its most passionate moments. But there are also moments of doubt and even of arrogance. At times we question with the same passion that moves us at other times to believe. We feel our power to be equal to that of anyone who might make claims on us through

actions or words. We deserve to be reckoned with. Enter J.

As suggested earlier, the Yahwist's story is not really a creation story at all. Whatever is 'created' in J has the quality of a set or a scene being built in which the real action will take place. God's creation waits upon what humans will do for it to become whatever it will be. God's power in this scene is potential. J then tells the story of the conflict between YHWH's authority (potential power) and human free will. As the story ends, we have more of a clarification than a resolution. We understand the conflict better as it emerges from the primeval haze, but the story of the conflict continues. The action of the human character and God's response has effectively moved the scene from paradise to the world of the audience. The primeval story becomes their story. God's authority as a transaction with human beings begins in paradise and continues in our world. J's narrative of God's power is necessarily incomplete.

We indicated earlier that P stands as an adjectival appendage to J. We can now see that adjectival relationship as embodying P's version of the interplay between the two dimensions of power. Without authorship, authority remains embroiled in the indeterminacy of conflict. There is no circumscribing force that can determine the outcome. Because human beings are not part of a completed vision of perfection, their action emanates from their own ambiguous nature and is not drawn towards a definite end. It unfolds in endless story.

P qualifies J by elaborating a claim that the universe is a perfectly ordered hierarchy, with God ruling over all as the only significant actor. He brings his account to a close with a statement which suggests that both the creation and the story have been completed perfectly: 'Such is the story of heaven and earth as they were created' (2.4a). This liturgical gloss has the ring of a claim. God created perfectly and the story of that creation has been perfectly told.

But P's account leaves God as author with nothing to do but 'uncreate' if his vision is significantly violated. This is, of course, precisely what happens in the flood story (Gen. 6-9). Humans have no creative potential of their own to serve as the basis for more story (other than the story of uncreation). P's vision of God's authorship thus forecloses any significant story that might follow. There is nothing more of interest that might happen. Perfection has realized itself.

By joining his account to J's, the Priestly Writer not only adds the circumscribing claim of authorship to J's story of God's authority,

but he also permits himself to make that claim in the perfect rhetoric that befits it. By introducing conflict rather than authorial creation as his primary motif, J provides that dimension of God's power which invites more story. J's account ends not with a claim of closure but with the scene set for the story of man in his 'fallen state'.

His subject, God's authority, leads the Yahwist to compose an 'imperfect rhetoric' that opens itself up to the future, just as P closes his account in the perfect past. Human actors and audiences can continue the story that God and J begin. God's authorship in P necessarily lacked the appeal to the questioning, active side of human beings. P leaves nothing for people as actors or audiences to do. J's narrative in Genesis has been recognized by critics as possessing a universal appeal, a claim not made about P. It is perhaps more accurate to say that J appeals to audiences in a wider range of mood than does P. P can offer only a vision of the perfect grandeur of God and the goodness of the created world to people who are in a mood receptive to such a vision. J leads his audience indirectly through a wide assortment of interpretive possibilities that can extend God's power to a more universal range of human experience.

So J apparently complements P's vision of power, just as P complements J's. But the complementarity of the two texts does not leave authorship and authority as equal partners with one another. As human beings live through the story of their relationship with God, their participation in creation is circumscribed by God's authorship. In the P-J text, authority is dialectically circumscribed by authorship. We call the circumscription dialectical because it arises out of the complementary interplay between authorship and authority in the two accounts.

One pole of the dialectic is represented in P by God's pronouncement that his creation is 'good'. God's authorship permits him to enact what he knows to be good and to judge it so. The other dialectical pole is acted out by Adam and Eve, according to their nature. They must try to realize the possibility of authorship, of becoming like God. Their achievement is realistically ambiguous. They know more than they did before, but they are at a loss about how to act on their knowledge. They know good and evil, but cannot be certain about the difference. They do not have the power of authorship wherein knowledge, act, and judgment are one. God's power as author circumscribes the power of human beings to transact with him as authority.

In J's story of God's authority, the human capacity to construct history through their own choices and actions is recognized. In P–J, the human construction of history (J's developing story) meets dialectically with God's perfectly created world (P's completed story). God's vision of perfection arises as the dominant force out of the P–J narrative. Human beings cannot engage the world presented to them as co-creators. God's authorship provides the 'true' construction of reality, which must be sought as the final arbiter of human action. God's original creation must eventually circumscribe human action. The dialectical circumscription of authority by authorship can thus be seen as the progenitor of eschatology. 'In the end it will be as it was in the beginning'.

Power and Rhetoric

We conclude that Genesis 1–3, P's *narratio* read as adjectivally appended to J's narration, is less about creation as such than about the dimensions of power. Our reading of the text strongly indicates that P's adjective of authorship dialectically circumscribes J's vision of God's power as authority. There are, of course, other possible readings. But we contend that they too would have to grow out of the dialectical relationship between the P and J accounts of power that can be found in the text. This relationship is dialectical in an Hegelian sense, as unity in opposition, a 'natural harmony' of opposites such that one cannot exist without the other: P's 'authorship' is the capacity to make and unmake. It is absolute, the kind of power that does not recognize human choice and does not brook, or even tolerate, the possibility of resistance, dissent, or conflict. It is self-willful, existing without equal or opposite will and with no notion even of the desirability of negotiation. It is perfect and permanent.

The Yahwist's 'authority' is the capacity to lead, advise, and inspire. It is relative to the choice of human beings to recognize it, and it unfolds across time in interaction or negotiation with others. The need to recognize others as agents capable of will themselves makes J's power more comfortable to bear and easier to exercise among those who respond favorably to leaders (and gods) who care. As a circular continuum, authorship to authority and back again, P's *narratio* and J's narration account for every possible form and function of divine power. God's place in human affairs will be determined by how people, as individuals or in groups, settle upon a

particular, formal conception of the relationship between authorship and authority, a point on the continuum.

But whatever point is chosen, however one constructs the 'ideal' relationship between authorship and authority, an ambiguity and a tension remain in the settlement. From one direction, human will pulls against acknowledgment that a deity has authored us; and from the other direction, knowledge that *genesis* is a biological fact (if it is nothing more) pulls against an always-unsure-of-itself human will. To escape the uncomfortable consequences of the human condition, we would like to be free and to be determined both at the same time, and we are necessarily unsure of how to manage that.

Now it is important that *genesis* is not just an interesting literary allusion to other Mesopotamian creation myths which also began, 'In the beginning'. In a sense, each human life is a reenactment of beginnings. Each child experiences the presence of giant parents who formulate mysterious rules, praise and punish, and who exist in relation to him/her literally as biological authors of existence. The feeling that Genesis 1-3 circumscribes a kind of truth seems to be a product of comparing the P and J narratives against our own primitive experiences in what Walter Benjamin describes as a 'dialectical engagement':

> To articulate the past historically does not mean to recognize it 'the way it really was' (Ranke). It means to seize hold of a memory as it flashes up at a moment of danger. Historical materialism wishes to retain that image of the past which unexpectedly appears to a man singled out by history at a moment of danger. The danger affects both the content of the tradition and its receivers. The same threat hangs over both.[19]

Genesis 1-3 purports to be more than sacred speculation about how God set the world in motion; it is *history*, an account of what happened in sacred time. It is to be taken as fact, established by the text in itself, not by documentary evidence, anthropological artifacts, or close textual comparisons with *Enuma Elish*. It captures an *image* of the way it was, and, like any figure, the image is recognized as accurate only as it touches deeply the experience of those who hear it. Biological *genesis* experienced by each individual stands as a ready touchstone to establish the propriety of any image of human origins generally. Thus there is a 'ring of truth' in Genesis 1-3 independent of its status as a sacred document or its context.

Even though it helps explain how the text resonates with truth,

this biological analogy remains only an interpretive metaphor. In fact, the Biblical authors were careful to avoid any suggestion of sexual generation in the terminology and accounts of creation. This was not due to a prudishness about sexuality, but to their doctrine of divine transcendence: God has no sexual gender, and there is no continuity between the being of God and the being of earthly creatures.

But this avoidance of any overt reference to biology leaves substantial interpretive space open for another significant resonance of the text's truth: namely, that it is historically material; that is, it has been taken for centuries as a figurative paradigm of social and political power. Genesis 1-3 not only brought certain universals of the human condition to light, it shaped the civilizations of the Near East and Europe through their theories of power. These theories are the rhetorical means by which rulers have legitimated their rule and revolutionaries have challenged their legitimacy.

Absolute monarchs such as James I of England, for example, described and justified their power as authorial, *like* God's:

> If you will consider the Attributes to God, you shall see how they agree in the person of a King. God hath power to create or destroy, make or unmake at his pleasure, to give life or send death, to judge all, and to be judged nor accountable to none. . . And the like power have Kings: they make and unmake their subjects; they have power of raising, and casting down; of life and of death; judges over all of their subjects, and in all causes, and yet accountable to none but God only. They have power to exalt low things, and abase high things, and make of their subjects like men at the Chess. A pawn to take a Bishop or a Knight, and to cry up or down any of their subjects as they do their money.[20]

The P-J narrative establishes a structure which could be used, and was used, to organize the facts of social existence in such a way as to justify the existence of human authors, Kings with the absolute power of a creator.

The argument is a fascinating and intricate tautology: Scripture is holy by decree, God's own word, and that decree is recognizably genuine because it 'rings true' against the shadowy memory of one's own biological *genesis*. The story is retold with Kings in place of God and subjects in place of Adam and Eve. This second account is recognizably genuine because it 'rings true' against the textualized memory of human origins recorded in Genesis 1-3. Consequent

acceptance of hierarchical social-political order makes Genesis 1–3 seem even more 'authentic' and the materially reinforced sacred text makes monarchy seem more 'natural'.

All contemporary governments derive in one way or another from an absolute monarchy justified in its power-claims by appeal to the sacred. A god or gods were said to 'authorize' the practice of treating a human agent as if she/he were the 'author' of his/her community. Since most modern governments have reformed that conception by diffusing power, it is common to think of power as beginning with authorship and gradually (or explosively) changing *in form* to authority. So it has been common to classify 'forms' of government on the basis of determining how much authorship remains, who the authors are, and describing the rhetorical gymnastics authors must practice to seduce the polity into attributing authority to the governmental system. Power thus becomes something one *has* in some proportion or another in relation to other members of one's society. And the reification is complete in that theorists rarely discuss the power of Kings any more, but instead suggest that *all* members of the polity *have* 'autonomy' in some degree and are simultaneously in some degree 'dependent'.

> All power relations, or relation of autonomy and dependence, are reciprocal: however wide the asymmetrical distribution of resources involved, all power relations manifest autonomy and dependence 'in both directions'. A person kept thoroughly confined and supervised, as an individual in a strait-jacket, perhaps has lost all capability of action, and is not a participant in reciprocal power-relation. But in all other cases. . . power relations are two-way. This accounts for the intimate tie between agency and suicide. Self-destruction is a (virtually) always-open option, the ultimate refusal that finally and absolutely cancels the oppressive power of others.[21]

This 'dialectic of control' is anchored in a fixed and incomplete idea of power, for it thinks of power only as negated, in regard to a motive to resist—power is that claim on behavior and belief that we would like to be able to negate. This notion is fixed on the history of the western resistance to claims of absolute monarchs and on the view that an inherently more 'legitimate' kind of power developed in consequence of altering the form of government. Such an idea is incomplete because it wrongly supposes that power is fixed in a structure, that, for example, the power of Kings was in reality as authorial as their rhetoric would have indicated.

Power can best be conceived as function—it is, in the Weber/ Parsons/Luhmann vocabulary, a generalized medium of communication.[22] A monarch's claim to 'absolute' power was 'rhetorical' in both senses of that word: It was figurative in the metaphor James I developed in arguing that temporal power is the mirror-image of God's power over all of creation. It was also persuasive, in the attempt to *seduce* a polity into granting authority and suppressing awareness that even the power of God is ultimately dependent upon acknowledgment of him by this or that Adam and Eve bound in the time and space of one or another garden.

Those who opposed such claims as that of James I were neither power-hungry, impious, nor opposed to power; rather, they wanted, and eventually insisted upon, power conceived and justified as authority. There was not so much a desire to re-*form* government as to re-*gain* the 'love and care' of another 'absolute' monarch, Elizabeth I:

> I do assure you that there is no prince that loveth his subjects better, or whose love can countervail our love... There will never queen sit in my seat with more zeal to my country, care to my subjects, and that will sooner with willingness yield and venture her life for your good and safety than myself. And though you have had and may have many princes more mighty and wise sitting in this seat, yet you never had or shall have any that will be more careful and loving. . . I know the title of a king is a glorious title; but assure yourself that the shining glory of princely authority hath not so dazzled the eyes of our understanding but that we will know and remember that we also are to yield an account of our actions before the Great Judge. . . For myself, I was never so much enticed with the glorious name of a king, or royal authority of a queen, as delighted that God hath made me His instrument to maintain His truth and glory, and to defend this kingdom, as I said, from peril, dishonour, tyranny, and oppression.[23]

Elizabeth claimed to be an authority exercising the remanded power of God; James claimed to be an author exercising his own god-like, autonomous power. The claims were made eight years apart and in the context of very nearly the same interpenetrating religious/ political/economic/social structure. In Michel Foucault's terms, it is significant that the two monarchs presented different 'bodies' to the polity, one exuding 'maleness' and the other undeniably 'feminine'.[24] But the difference is not merely between matriarchy and patriarchy, for these are but flip sides of the same coin, the idea of parentage and

the power of *genesis*. The significant difference is a matter of *rhetorical style*: One cannot in fact *have* power; rather, even Kings *do* power by creating discourse that manages the contradiction between authorship and authority. No matter what form society assumes, power relations within it are determined by the need to cooperate, not the need to resist. That is, a polity must be persuaded not to resist, and such persuasion proceeds from some combination of appeals to *genesis* and simultaneous acknowledgment of the human will as it exists independent of its origins or parentage.

The problem with a reified idea of allegedly 'pure' power is its lack of *authenticity* or 'genuineness'. Each of us has internalized an idea of parentage and recognizes a 'right' deriving from it—a right to obedience at one stage of life, honor and respect at another. This right is 'authentic' when claimed by real parents who behave as we are taught to think parents should behave. The fact of parentage (authorship) is consonant with perceptions of parentage (authority), and we are bound in the power of *genesis*. When those who are not parents try to treat us *like* 'sons/daughters', the claim to authorship is inauthentic on its face, and power is wholly dependent on authority. And when those who are parents do not act the part, the claim to authority is on its face inauthentic, and power is wholly dependent on authorship. It is never in the interest of power-users to characterize their power as wholly authorial because the claim of a King to be 'father to his people', or of a Henry Ford to be 'head of the family', or of the Presidium 'to speak for' the people of the Soviet Union is always literally false, a metaphor always subject to unmasking *as* a metaphor. So James I felt the bitterness of metaphorical 'sons and daughters' who saw nothing at all father-like or god-like in his behavior. Similarly, it is never in the interest of power-users to characterize their power as entirely authoritative, for it is the radical perception of *parentage* that makes a claim to 'know better what is good for you' credible. The claim to love and care is easy to make, even by gigolos and harlots, but it is believable only from the mouth of one who is perceived as father/mother/'god'. So Elizabeth I was devilled by the charge that she was a 'bastard' and had no 'legitimate' claim to the throne—and, in light of her rhetorical style, no 'legitimate' claim to the rights of parentage. Authentic power, exercised in or on any social-political structure, emphasizes the fact of parentage when authorship may be doubted and parental behavior when authority may be doubted—and in either case, the goal of the rhetoric is to create a unity of power such that no

metaphorical 'son' or 'daughter' would think to resist any more than real daughters and sons would think to strike an aged and loving parent.

The true 'dialectic of control', we conclude, is the same as that circumscribed in the P and J narratives of human origins. 'Authorship' and 'authority' have meaning only in relationship to one another and in the context of the omnipresent problem of *genesis*, a problem reproduced biologically as each generation grows from the awe-ful dependence of a child to the relatively will-ful 'autonomy' of an adult, from the innocence of Adam and Eve to the knowledge-ability of Cain and Abel.

There are two perspectives from which to consider this dialectic: One could believe that J, and particularly P, were extraordinarily insightful or divinely inspired in constructing a sacred narrative that successfully circumscribed all possibilities of power, divine and profane. Such an interpretation would emphasize the structural repetition of the P/J dialectic in all times and situations where power exists—power would be functional, tied to discourse, in that it derives from the bio-logic of the human condition *per se*, not from the form and structure of institutions.

One could also believe that Genesis 1-3 is historically material, the point of embarkation for all western governments and, in consequence, for all western theories of power. Such an interpretation would emphasize the largely forgotten role of Judeo-Christian religion in establishing the practices of power about which we theorize—power in this view would be functional, tied to discourse, in that it originates in much-quoted and oft-reproduced sacred narratives, not in the present shape and structure of society.

For our present purposes, the result is the same: Whether Genesis 1-3 is 'sacred' because it captures the logic of a human condition or materially determinant because it has been taken as 'sacred', it is nonetheless an accurate, 'authentic' account of power as it now exists and as it has existed in western cultures. Power *does* rather than *is*. One does not have it by virtue of a 'place' within the social-political structure so much as one creates it as a rhetoric that must be performed within the possibilities of the authorship/authority dialectic.[25]

Chapter 7

'THE BIBLE SAYS. . .'

Everyone reading this has probably heard or read sentences of this construction countless times. Indeed, some of us may have uttered such sentences. They sound innocent enough, but they raise a difficult logical problem. If one means only that 'somewhere in the Bible it says. . .', we can simply hunt around and see. The logical conundrum arises when we ascribe this teaching to the whole of Scripture.

At one time that seemed to be no problem, for the divine author of Scripture guaranteed the consistency of its teaching. This assumption may still operate for many laymen and a few scholars. But critical scholarship has put a chink in such reasoning. Even in the pre-critical era, sophisticated interpreters recognized that there were apparent discrepancies within Scripture which need to be smoothed over by deft elucidation. Critical scholars seized upon the discrepancies to build a much more human picture of the book. Now we must recognize that each writing is an expression of one author, at one moment in time, with one point of view, not a representative of the Bible as a whole.

The question of the unity of Scripture gained a much higher degree of urgency when interpreters could no longer *presuppose* that Scripture exemplified the perfect consistency of the divine mind. Those who defended the revelatory character of the Bible had to *show* that there was some underlying or overarching unity which was divinely revealed. A conceptual scheme had to be worked out which in principle accounted for every passage of Scripture.

The most eloquent spokesman for this position among Old Testament theologians was probably Walther Eichrodt. It was his contention that

> there is one task which OT theology can never abandon, namely,
> that of pressing on from the evidence to a system of faith which
> shall, by reason of its unified structure and consistent fundamental
> attitude, present a character unique in the history of religions.[1]

He discerned this unified, consistent structure in the concept of
covenant; all the teaching of Scripture could be subsumed under the
covenant between YHWH and Israel, or the covenant between God
and the world, or God and 'man'.[2]

Over against the apologists for Scripture were hard-headed critics
who stressed its diversity of viewpoints. In the battle of ideologies,
these scholars were able to avoid the identification of any core of true
doctrine. In the place of revelation the critics of the nineteenth
century placed the development of ideas—a development that had an
inner cultural logic.

During the last quarter of the nineteenth century and the first
decade or so of the twentieth, the pluralists seem to have had the
upper hand. Then neo-orthodoxy fueled a rebellion among theologically inclined Biblical scholars. If Scripture is the Word of God, it
must—since it is self-evident that eternal truth be coherent and
unchanging—have a single, unified message.

Our own mentors shared the mindset of the neo-orthodox era and
were members of the 'movement' for a history-based Biblical
theology. They perceived the vulnerability of Eichrodt's maximal
claims for system, but they shared the conviction that there was an
underlying unity to scriptural teaching and that the task of the
theological interpreter was to uncover it.

Then came the 1960s—the 'death of God' theology, the seemingly
devastating critique of Biblical theology, and the various forms of
radicalism springing from the civil rights and anti-war movements.
The unifying conceptions of the Biblical theology movement—
covenant, kingdom of God, and saving history—became so suspect
that practically no one in tune with the times ventured to mention
them in scholarly conversation. The very search for a comprehensive
scheme of theological concepts and principles was disparaged.

Our objective in this chapter is to examine the possibilities in the
rhetorical approach for reversing this trend, or at least to state a
compelling case for synthesis. The argument will not be based upon
the hermeneutics of theologians like Eichrodt and others of the neo-
orthodox era; they tended to consider the question of unity to be
objective, a fact inherent in the text. Their opponents argued in like

manner that there were irreconcilable theological differences within the Bible. Our argument is based upon the rhetorical shaping of the text and the sort of reader required to give the claims of the text their proper due. The issue is, in our opinion, not one of fact, but of how the text rhetorically indicates it should be read.[3]

We wish to restrict the thesis to the Old Testament because it is an independent book with an integrity of its own and has an interpretative community that recognizes it as sufficient, when supplemented by oral tradition, for faith and practice. The relationship between the Old Testament and the New, and between Judaism and Christianity, should be kept separate from the question of unity.

The discussion will be concerned with the theological unity of the Old Testament; other possible unities will not be considered. By theology, we mean the type of discourse which speaks of a universal and eternal reality which is both transcendent of and immanent in the spacio-temporal universe. In the Old Testament this sort of discourse is more often presented in the form of narrative and histrionic utterances than logical propositions,[4] and it has a strong thrust toward eliciting the reader's belief and obedience.

E Pluribus Unum

The argument properly begins with reflections on the nature of the Old Testament. Although the book has the appearance of an anthology, it was not regarded as such by the Jewish community which originally accorded it the status of Scripture or the Christian church which adopted it.[5] Rather, the writings were understood to constitute a consistent communication of God to his people. Any passage could be cited as representative of the whole and all discrepancies were considered to be apparent only.

In the precritical era, of course, the multiplicity and diversity of authors of the text was not recognized. There was in fact an incipient historical criticism before the Enlightenment. The Antiochene school of interpretation in late antiquity, Rashi and his students in the Middle Ages, the school of St. Victor in the same era, and many of the Protestant reformers insisted that interpretation should remain faithful to the original, literal meaning of the text.

It took the Enlightenment's skepticism toward tradition, however, to question the ascriptions of authorship and challenge the harmonizing modes of exegesis dominant in the religious communities. For our question, it was the establishment of theological diversity in

Scripture which was most important. This arose to a great extent as a corollary of source analysis, which seeks out the discrepancies in a text.

To establish the pluralism of the Bible, critical scholarship had to dismantle the collecting and editing work of the anonymous 'redactors' who combined the various sources representing divergent viewpoints into one text. There was initially little appreciation among critical scholars for the accomplishment of these scribes of old. Their effect upon the text was considered to be in the order of censorship, and badly executed as well.

Canonical Criticism
Recently the work of the scribes who passed on and shaped the extant text has been re-evaluated. There is a growing appreciation of their intellectual and artistic achievement. Their work was to select writings from Yahwistic tradition and organize and integrate them into a single authoritative book for the religious life of the Jewish people. It was their achievement to blend the voices of the tradition together to form a choir.

Our thesis is that we need not only to focus scholarly interest on the synthetic work of these traditionists—often designated the 'canonical process'—but also to develop its theological import. That import is, we will argue, that the scriptural text is shaped to be read as a unified teaching.

Admittedly, the full implications of 'canonical criticism' are still in dispute. One of the leaders of this new level of inquiry, James Sanders, draws quite different conclusions from the canonical process:

> Canonical criticism celebrates the pluralism of the Bible and stresses its self-critical dimension in the varied thrusts and statements it records. There is no program that can be constructed on the basis of the Bible which can escape the challenge of other portions of it: this is an essential part of its pluralism.[6]

One can see how canonical criticism can reinforce our recognition of the diversity of scriptural writings and encourage us to accord the dissidents' dissonance a special hearing. Canonical criticism did not discover these qualities of our text, but it does provide a new perspective on the existence of theological pluralism. We now see a community which was amazingly open to diversity, respectful of competing theological visions, resistant to reductionistic unity.

However, the redactors and editors did not regard the pluralism of their sources as irreducible. The extant text is replete with synthetic devices. Narratives from different authors are sometimes juxtaposed to balance extreme positions, e.g., the creation text in Genesis 1-2[7] and the account of the founding of the monarchy in 1 Samuel 7-12; sometimes woven together into one continuous account, e.g., the account of the great flood in Genesis 5-9[8] and the call of Moses in Exodus 3-4; sometimes repeated to interpret each other, e.g., the endangering of the matriarch in Genesis 12, 20 and 26.[9] The prophetic books were edited and supplemented to integrate the specific message of the individual prophet into the common prophetic message.[10] Amos, for example, has oracles of salvation appended to his message of doom to conform to the message of his fellow prophets. Even such free-thinking writings as Ecclesiastes and Job were tamed by subsequent readers and thereby integrated into the dialectical unity of Scripture.[11]

Sanders's irreducible pluralism swims against the stream of the canonical process. Brevard Childs is surely correct to regard that flow as in the direction of synthesis.[12] The *Tradenten* were seeking to blend the diverse traditions into a unified presentation of God's history with Israel against the background of his history with all creation. It was assumed that readers, under the prompting of their rhetorical signals, would finish the process of synthesis in the act of interpretation.

The most telling objection to Childs's canonical criticism is that the synthetic work of the redactors, editors and commentators is not regulative for our interpretation. Why should we give precedence to the amalgamators of the tradition? They are surely no more authoritative for us than the original authors.[13]

While this observation may well be valid, it does not defeat the thesis that the canonical process was synthetic. It may also be a bit misleading by isolating the canonical process from the compositional process. All too often critical scholars have regarded canonization as something that happened to the writings long after they were written. The canonical process, however, cannot be limited to the final assemblage of the sacred text, but was operative throughout the history of tradition. The earliest pentateuchal narratives incorporated even older material and soon were expanded and redacted in turn, and a similar process is identifiable in the other segments of the canon. It is just this practice of assimilating and qualifying diverse writings that yielded the canon that we know.

The authors themselves were a part of the canonical process. They did not set themselves off from the tradition as independent creative geniuses. This is demonstrated by their studied anonymity and their treatment of tradition. They depended upon tradition for their presentations, they incorporated and alluded to other works, and they endeavored to articulate a public faith. One can surmise that they offered their own works to the community as an extension of the tradition already known and allowed the bearers of that tradition to assess the fittingness of their writing to the common faith and life.[14] In other words, they sought to blend into the choir.

This does not mean, of course, that the works of these authors blended in without a trace. Critical scholars are quite right to reconstruct the highly original artistic and theological statements of individual authors, the conflicting streams of tradition within the culture, and the ideological coloring of the common tradition due to the social location of the author. The pluralism is evident and should not be obscured.

However, this pluralism was not perceived by the bearers of tradition as irreducible. Jon Levenson states this point well in his conclusions regarding the Zion/David and Sinai/Covenant traditions:

> ... it is an overstatement to present them as always standing in sharp and irreconcilable antithesis. We have already noted that Davidic circles were quite capable of accepting and redacting literature that had originally no place for David but a central place for Moses, for example, the book of Hosea. There may be a tension in the final product of such redaction, but the tension was tolerable to the proponents of Judean royalism.[15]

It may even be the case that the tensions are intended as a constituent element of what is communicated. That is, the *Tradenten* may have designed to text to be read dialectically, bringing together points of view which oppose or at least pass by each other. If this is the case, the reader who rejects synthesis is not fathoming all the text has to say.

To sum up, the bearers of the Old Testament traditions shaped them to read as one communication of God. This canonical process was synthetic. It was operative throughout the history of the tradition. The authors of the works were a part of the process and acknowledged the authority of tradition over their individual works. The works accepted into the orthodox Yahwistic tradition were quite diverse, producing many tensions and discontinuities, but the

bearers of tradition did not perceive them as incompatible when they were read correctly.

The Theological Stakes

It is time to consider the theological issue at stake in the debate between synthesists and pluralists. The decisive truth-claim of the Old Testament is articulated in the first commandment: 'You shall have no other gods before (besides) me'. Not only is Israel forbidden commerce with any deity but YHWH, YHWH promises Israel that they will be dealing with him alone.

This principle is built into the structure of Biblical literature. The Old Testament story accords the status of deity to YHWH alone. It is this God who is depicted and described in the Pentateuch, Former and Latter Prophets, Psalms and wisdom literature. The names of other deities are mentioned from time to time, but never are any portrayed as active, independent agents in the process of nature or the drama of human affairs. For all practical purposes, the Old Testament is monotheistic.[16]

The argument that the Old Testament is irreducibly and irreconcilably pluralistic in its theologies would seriously undermine this apparent monotheism. It would mean that the authors of our literature shared only the belief in the existence of one God and an agreement to name this deity YHWH.[17] If there is no common identity to the one deity named YHWH, Biblical monotheism must be adjudged an empty shell.

This argument can be cast historically. Biblical literature depicts YHWH as the sovereign Lord of all times and places. In the segment of history recounted in the Old Testament—from primeval events through the call of Abraham down to the exile and return—he has made himself known to Israel from generation to generation. If, however, the theological witnesses of Scripture are as incompatibly diverse as it is alleged, YHWH has not manifested himself with any consistency. He simply is not one and the same God from age to age.

The Old Testament makes its claim that YHWH is the same from age to age and tradition to tradition not only by explicit assertion, but by thrusting before us texts representative of different ages and interests. All of them bear witness to the God whom alone Israel is to recognize.[18] To recognize this God, the reader must proceed dialectically through these various witnesses in search of the One whose identity remains the same. It is only as the interpreter takes up

this task that he or she can grasp the 'truth' the text has to communicate.

The Ideal Reader

What sort of reader did the authors and redactors need for their writing and editing to communicate most effectively what they offer? Such a reader can be called the text's 'ideal reader'. James Boyd White offers this definition of that term: 'For me, the most valuable way to talk about the 'meaning' of a text is to ask, among other things, what version of himself or herself it invites the reader to become: that is, to focus attention upon what I call its "ideal reader"'.[19] This would have, first of all, to do with the way the reader relates to the communication of the text itself; we might say that the ideal reader is the one who is willing to interpret the text as the best text it can be.

It is clear from the way that the text combines sources that the reader is expected to complete the synthesis which has been inaugurated by the redactors and editors. Genesis 1 was meant to be read in conjunction with Genesis 2, each text qualifying the other's depiction of the Creator.[20] These in turn were to be assimilated to passages in the Psalms, Prophets, etc., which portray creation. While the modern critical scholar concentrates on the distinctive communication of each text, the canonical shaping of the text calls upon the reader to synthesize the texts into one unified conception of the Creator and creation.

However, the role of ideal reader cannot be a passive, subservient one. If the text deserves our attention, it should encourage truth-seeking. The synthesis that the redaction of Scripture inaugurates may not make the Bible the best text it can be. The text may come to life better if its diversity is not obscured, but left to witness to a God who eludes all human schemes of coherence. The process of qualifying one witness by another may level the profound and the mundane, the disinterested and the ideological, and so forth.

In the remainder of this section, we will take up three arguments for resisting the synthetic shaping of the text, and offer a rebuttal. Our counter-arguments will constitute our case in behalf of synthesis.

The Case for Critical Deconstruction

Does the synthesis encouraged by the shaping of the text obscure the

distinctive viewpoints of the writings which were redacted? One would have to answer that the harmonistic exegesis of the pre-critical era did in fact 'level' the text. It has been the genuine achievement of critical scholarship to recover the individuality of passages and their authors. Who would be willing to relinquish the particular voice of Isaiah of Jerusalem or the anonymous prophet Second Isaiah?

However, the necessity of abandoning the traditional devices for harmonizing the witnesses of Scripture does not invalidate the endeavor to devise unifying schemes compatible with a critical vantage point. In fact, modern Biblical scholarship and theology are replete with unifying schemes. Developmental and evolutionary schemes were once quite popular, and theologians were able to set this sort of scheme out under the rubric of 'progressive revelation'. Though the scheme was flawed, it did its service and continues to contribute some important insights into texts.

The process of the formation and amalgamation of traditions has had great appeal in this century. It functions as a synthetic scheme for scholars as diverse as von Rad and Levenson. Indeed, canonical criticism operates on this model, and Fishbane's studies of 'intertextuality' appear to fit here as well.[21] Whether it will prove durable only time will tell.

The new movement that goes by the name, 'the literary approach', is already challenging it.[22] If the most militant exponents of this approach have their way, a formalistic, synchronic mode of interpretation will play the primary role in exegesis, with source and traditio-historical criticism relegated to an extra-exegetical role.[23] This study of the artistic design and evocative power of the extant text has the capacity to provide a unified picture of the Biblical message.[24] If one proceeds systematically to put together what the source critics had dismembered, it would seem natural and logical to extend the synthetic reading of composite texts to the whole of the Old Testament.

The interpretation of the text as a rhetorical exchange between a text and its audiences may provide a way to synthesize the diachronic modes of interpretation that have dominated critical scholarship until recently and the synchronic modes of interpretation establishing their legitimacy now. The Biblical theologian is hardly without avenues of synthesis which are compatible with the critical understanding of the multiplicity and diversity of the voices in Scripture.

The possibility of legitimate synthesis is available; the interpreter can fulfill the role the text has designed for the reader.[25] That role is to complete the synthesis inaugurated by the authors and redactors of Biblical literature. Theologically, the claim that YHWH is one can be recognized without denying or obscuring the rich diversity of theologies uncovered by critical scholarship.

The Case for Pluralism

History has shown that the commitment to articulating a consistent, comprehensive divine communication in Scripture has not yielded unanimity among interpreters. There is an essential disagreement between Jews and Christians over the message of the Hebrew Scripture/Old Testament, and within Judaism and Christianity there are persistent disputes over the meaning of texts to which all parties appeal. The quest for a unified revelation of God has been decidedly divisive.

One might conclude that the religious communities would have been better off if they had recognized that Scripture is pluralistic and incapable of synthesis. Indeed, it is possible that the pluralism of the religious communities reflects the pluralism of Scripture.[26]

That, however, would have made no sense to them, for they were seeking the sort of comprehensive, consistent revelation which is necessary to monotheistic faith. To trust and obey God, a believer must know God to be faithful to his promises and righteous in his commandments. An inconsistent or fragmentary communication from God would undermine the capacity to be trusting and obedient. Of course, a certain kind of piety would still be possible, as is evidenced in polytheism, with its arbitrary, unpredictable and contradictory divinities. Monotheism, however, purports to transform piety toward the mysterious forces that impinge on human life into faith in one sovereign, self-consistent (faithful) Creator and Redeemer.

Until recently, the religious communities believed that their Scriptures met the requirements of monotheistic faith. The prospective Presbyterian minister, for example, was asked to affirm that 'the Scriptures of the Old and New Testaments (are) the word of God, the only infallible rule of faith and practice'. The candidate was then called upon to avow his church's confessions and catechisms as articulating 'the system of doctrine taught in Holy Scripture'.[27] Although other communions were not always so explicit, practically all Jews and Christians assumed that their Scripture was a consistent

and comprehensive revelation of God and that their communion articulated that revelation in its doctrines and traditions.

Such affirmations may sound quaint and naive in our sophisticated, skeptical and pluralistic age. We need not, however, reject the theological necessity of synthesis because an older era was too absolutist and objectivist in its claims for its doctrines. We could acknowledge that the search for the consistent, comprehensive communication of God in Scripture is legitimate, but confess that this communication is too elusive to be fixed in any system of thought or interpretive tradition. Religious communities should recognize the finitude and historical conditioning of their traditions and creeds and confess that the truth which they have heard is distorted by their 'heavy ears'.[28] Every synthesis is for a particular time and community and is to be measured by the faithfulness of its witness to God in that context. No synthesis is timeless, though every faithful witness enriches the understanding of later generations.

The need of religious communities for synthesis is consonant with the rhetorical shaping of Scripture. The excesses of the past can be avoided if the synthesis is pursued with a sensitivity to the rhetorical nature of textual communication. The incipient relativism of this understanding can be counterbalanced by the adoption of the interpretive dictum, interpret the text as the best text it can be. This dictum interjects seriousness into the quest for a unified message while reminding the interpreter that no one can be certain that the best text has been found.

The Case for Interpretive Freedom
Those who oppose synthesis still have an argument in their favor. The text has meant a lot of different things to a lot of different people over time. Why must we close off this fecundity by insisting on a single, true meaning? Why not allow interpreters the freedom to find whatever values they can from their reading of the text?

This is not, strictly speaking, an argument against synthesis, but an argument against any norm of interpretation. However, it can be applied to the question of synthesis. The freedom to garner whatever values one can find in the Scripture would entail the freedom to select passages that claim one's conscience and ignore the rest, and to interpret those passages without considering how they have been qualified by others.

If we were to formulate this argument in terms of the dictum that we should interpret the Bible as the best book it can be, it would run

something like this: The Bible really does not make a very good synthesis, but it makes a good source of fragmentary insights into the human condition. When it is synthesized, the brilliant insights of particular passages are muted and obscured and sinful and incompetent writings are given weight that they should not have. The Bible is the best text it can be when it is allowed to engender whatever reading the interpreter gives it.

This argument has traditionally been thought to be vulnerable because of its subjectivism or arbitrariness. However, our contemporary respect for freedom of conscience seriously weakens the force of this sort of objection. The authority of Scripture cannot be imposed from outside, but must be found in the inner compellingness of its message.

We believe that the practice of conscientious interpretation counts against the belief that best text of Scripture is a collection of fragmentary insights. If the reader finds a given text's claims compelling, he or she will more or less spontaneously correlate these claims with those of other texts of equal compellingness. One naturally assumes that the compelling passages are congruent with each other, and that the interpreter can, when the occasion arises, articulate a comprehensive scheme of concepts and principles covering passages which appeal to the interpreter's conscience.

What happens when the interpreter discovers texts which he or she believes to misrepresent God or falsify the human condition? A properly engaged reader will inquire further to determine whether the text in fact means what it seemed to mean on initial reading. If further exchanges with the text do not find 'the best text it can be' to be good enough, it behooves the interpreter to exercise judgment.

What is the standard of the judgment to be applied? Let us not be dishonest here: One's judgment will be—and should be—based on personal moral and religious convictions. However, these convictions have no exegetical status; to give one's judgments exegetical status, one must show that the offending text is not consistent with the texts one finds compelling. The latter function as the interpreter's synthetic perception of the 'essential teaching of Scripture'.

What this description of exegetical practice has shown is that the truth-claims of Scripture about God require a dialectical synthesis of the texts that render YHWH. The interpreter naturally brings together compelling passages in a working synthesis and judges other passages by their consistency or inconsistency with that synthetic scheme of the theological teaching of Scripture.

There are bound to be disputes among Biblical theologians over the essential teaching of Scripture regarding the one God recognized from age to age and tradition to tradition. Such disputes are not incorrigible, for interpretative standards—comprehensiveness, consistency, cogency and profundity—can be applied.[29] A conscientious interpreter will be willing to join the discussion over the most profound and compelling understanding of the theological message of Scripture and expand or change his or her views when the discussion so warrants.

Conclusions

In the course of our argument we have found that the Old Testament traditions were shaped to be read as one communication of God. The works accepted into the orthodox Yahwistic tradition were quite diverse, producing many tensions and discontinuities, but the bearers of tradition integrated them in such a way that the reader would be led to synthesize them.

The oneness of the God of Israel is at stake in this rhetorically elicited synthesis of the diverse writings of the Old Testament. The text makes its claim that YHWH is the same from age to age and tradition to tradition not only by explicit assertion, but by preserving texts representative of different ages and interests. All of them witness to the God whom alone Israel is to recognize. To recognize this God, the reader must proceed dialectically through these various witnesses in search of the One whose identity remains the same. It is only as the interpreter takes up this task that he or she can appreciate the 'truth' the text has to communicate.

The synthesis of the diverse theologies of Scripture should be consonant with the findings of critical scholarship; there are several compelling models for synthesis, not the least of them being the rhetorical understanding of the text developed in this volume. Though the claims to possess the true understanding of Scripture have been a divisive force in the history of Judaism and Christianity, a religious community needs to seek a synthesis to be faithful to the God of Scripture. The inordinate claims of the past can be avoided by a sensitivity to the rhetorical nature of textual communication and by the adoption of the best text principle to guide interpretation. The need for theological synthesis should not violate the conscience of the interpreter, but in fact can be seen as the natural practice of a conscientious scholar-theologian.

NOTES

Notes to Preface

1. Gadamer calls this alternative 'strengthening'. He observes that in this process, 'What is said is continually transformed into the uttermost possibilities of its rightness and truth and overcomes all opposing argument which seeks to limit its validity' (*Truth and Method* [trans. Garrett Barden and John Cumming; New York: Continuum, 1975], p. 331).

2. Reprinted in the *Journal of Biblical Literature* 88/1 (March 1969), pp. 1-18.

Notes to Chapter 1

1. Muilenburg, 'Form Criticism and Beyond'.

2. *Ibid.*, p. 18.

3. *Ibid.*, p. 18.

4. For an explication of this broader understanding, see especially George Kennedy, *Classical Rhetoric and its Christian and Secular Tradition from Ancient to Modern Times* (Chapel Hill: The University of North Carolina Press, 1980).

5. *The Rhetoric of Aristotle* (trans. Lane Cooper; New York: Appleton Century Crofts, 1932), 1354 a.

6. See, especially, Hans Georg Gadamer, *Truth and Method*, and Richard Rorty, *Philosophy and the Mirror of Nature* (Princeton, N.J.: Princeton University Press, 1979).

7. Robert L. Scott, 'On Viewing Rhetoric as Epistemic', *Central States Speech Journal* 18 (1967), pp. 9-17.

8. It should be noted, as well, that we have expanded the scope of the concept of rhetoric when we use it for written texts. Classical rhetoric focused upon public speaking and written correspondence. By this narrow definition, rhetoric would be only marginally useful in Old Testament interpretation, for only prophetic speeches and perhaps wisdom instruction would fall within its scope. Modern scholars of rhetoric, and literary critics have expanded the range of rhetoric to include the ways authors of narratives construct the relationship to their readers. It is the broadened definition with which we will operate.

9. Kenneth Burke, *A Rhetoric of Motives* (Berkeley: University of California Press, 1969).

10. Muilenburg, pp. 2-3.

11. *Ibid.*, p. 5.

12. *Ibid.*, pp. 2-3.

13. *Ibid.*, p. 6.

14. *Ibid.*, p. 5.

15. *Ibid.*, p. 9.

16. *Ibid.*, p. 2.

17. This idea is phrased in the language of Kenneth Burke; see especially *The Rhetoric of Motives* (Berkeley: University of California Press, 1969), pp. 37-40.

18. Gadamer expresses this idea, originally formulated by Schleiermacher, in a number of places; see, for example, 'Rhetoric, Hermeneutics, and the Critique of Ideology: Metacritical Comments on Truth in Method', in Kurt Mueller-Vollmer, ed., *The Hermeneutics Reader* (New York: Continuum, 1985), pp. 274-92.

19. Cf. his remarks on Jeremiah 3.1-4.4 (Muilenburg, p. 5).

20. The rhetorical critics cannot be given sole credit for this turn toward the extant text. It seems, rather, that scholars in various parts of the world, practicing various methods, came to the same conclusion at approximately the same time. Brevard Childs' version of canonical criticism has arrived at the same conclusion by another route, viz., via tradition history.

21. Two scholars from outside the discipline of Biblical scholarship have made this point forcefully in recent years: Michael Walzer, *Exodus and Revolution* (New York: Basic Books, 1985), and Northrop Frye, *The Great Code* (New York: Harcourt, Brace, Jovanovich, 1982), pp. xvi-xix, and throughout.

22. So Meir Sternberg, *The Poetics of Biblical Narrative* (Bloomington: Indiana University Press, 1985) pp. 7-8, 35.

23. Robert Alter, *The Art of Biblical Narrative* (New York: Basic Books, 1981).

24. *Ibid.*, p. 176.

25. Sternberg, *The Poetics of Biblical Narrative*.

26. In addition to Gadamer, another example is Paul Ricoeur who has been a keynote speaker at several SBL/AAR Annual Meetings in the last decade.

27. Thus Ronald Beiner's interpretation of Aristotle's concept of *homonoia* developed in Chapter 6 of Book 9 of the *Ethics*. Ronald Beiner, *Political Judgment* (Chicago: University of Chicago Press, 1983), p. 80.

28. Quoted by Beiner, p. 18.

29. Dworkin, Ronald, *A Matter of Principle* (Cambridge: Harvard University Press, 1985), p. 149.

30. See the discussion in Chapter 5, 'Finding the Best Job'.

31. For an example of this in operation, see the discussion in Chapter 6, 'Genesis and Power'. This chapter was originally published in a somewhat different form by Allen Scult, Michael Calvin McGee, and J. Kenneth Kuntz: 'Genesis and Power: An Analysis of the Biblical Story of Creation', *Quarterly Journal of Speech* 72 (May, 1986), pp. 113-31.

Notes to Chapter 2

1. George Kennedy, *Classical Rhetoric and its Christian and Secular Tradition from Ancient to Modern Times*, p. 5.

2. *Ibid.*, p. 120.

3. Origen, *On First Principles* (trans. G.W. Butterworth; New York: Harper and Row, 1966), p. 267.

4. *On Christian Doctrine* (trans. D.W. Robertson, Jr; Indianapolis: Library of Liberal Arts, 1958), 4. 8. 22.

5. The program for rhetorical criticism as the delineation of genres is found in Muilenburg's essay.

6. See Henry Fischel, 'Story and History: Observations on Greco-Roman Rhetoric and Pharisaism', in Henry A. Fischel, ed., *Essays in Greco-Roman and Related Talmudic Literature* (New York: Ktav, 1977), pp. 443-72.

7. Kennedy, p. 6.

8. See, especially, *Enuma Elish*, trans. by E.A. Speiser, in James Pritchard, ed., *Ancient Near Eastern Texts Related to the Old Testament* (Princton: Princeton University Press, 1955), pp. 60-72.

9. In Enuma Elish, after a battle amongst the gods, man is fashioned by the victor out of the blood of one of the losing combatants. Regarding man's function in the scheme of things, the text says the following: 'The savage man...[is to] ... be charged with the service of the gods that they may be at ease' (*Enuma Elish*, p. 68).

10. The Hebrew *'tov méod'* in this context suggests something like 'perfect'. This exegetical insight was communicated orally by Professor E.A. Speiser in his seminar on Genesis, University of Pennsylvania, Fall, 1963.

11. Lloyd Bitzer, 'The Rhetorical Situation', *Philosophy and Rhetoric* (1968), p. 6.

12. See for example the introduction to the Ten Commandments: 'I am the Lord your God who brought thee out of the Land of Egypt, out of the House of Bondage...' (Exod. 20.2).

13. Robert Alter rehearses this evidence and discusses its significance in his *Art of Biblical Narrative*.

14. Hayden White, 'The Value of Narrativity in the Representation of Reality' in W.J.T. Mitchell, ed., *On Narrative* (Chicago: University of Chicago Press, 1981), pp. 1-23.

15. *Ibid.*, p. 20.

16. The Rabbis took this command in Exod. 13.9 literally and so instituted the tradition of the teffilin which have boxes containing the story of the Exodus which are put on the head and forearm.

17. Quoted in Susan A. Handleman, *The Slayers of Moses: The Emergence of Rabbinic Interpretation in Modern Literary Theory* (Albany: State University of New York Press, 1982), p. 30.

18. This idea is expressed a number of times in the Talmud. See Handleman, pp. 40f., for examples.

19. The idea is discussed by Hans Georg Gadamer in a number of places. For an excellent discussion of it see David Linge's introduction to Gadamer's *Philosophical Hermeneutics* (Berkeley: University of California Press, 1976), pp. xix-xx.

20. See especially Fischel.

21. Ellis Rivkin makes a strong argument for a discontinuity between the Bible and Rabbinic interpretation in his *Shaping Jewish History* (New York: Scribners, 1971)

22. See Gadamer, *Truth and Method*, p. 364.

23. 'Gadamer's Theory of Interpretation' in E.D. Hirsch, *Validity in Interpretation* (New Haven: Yale University Press, 1967), pp. 245-264.

24. Alasdair MacIntyre, *After Virtue* (Notre Dame: University of Notre Dame Press, 1981), p. 201.

25. *Ibid.*, p. 211.

26. Max Kadushin, *The Rabbinic Mind* (New York: The Jewish Theological Seminary of America, 1952), p. 142.

27. Matthew Arnold, *Literature and Dogma* (London: Macmillan, 1892), p. 52.

Notes to Chapter 3

1. Hans Frei, *The Eclipse of Biblical Narrative* (New Haven: Yale University Press, 1974), p. 16.

2. White rehearses this argument in a number of places: see, for example, his essay, 'The Value of Narrativity in the Representation of Reality'.

3. It is noteworthy that Gerhard von Rad's epoch-making essay, 'The Form-Critical Problem of the Hexateuch', available in English in *The Problem of the Hexateuch and Other Essays* (Edinburgh and London: Oliver & Boyd, 1966), pp. 1-78, builds upon these two passages.

4. Susan Suleiman, *Authoritarian Fictions* (New York: Columbia University Press, 1983), p. 54.

5. See, especially, his *Rhetoric of Motives*, pp. 20ff.

6. The ways that narratives make and support their arguments are explored by Walter R. Fisher, *Human Communication as Narration* (Columbia: University of South Carolina, 1987).

7. Robert Alter, *The Art of Biblical Narrative*.

8. Quoted in John Van Seters, *In Search of History* (New Haven: Yale University, 1983), p. 1.

9. The term and the idea come from Michael Polanyi, *The Tacit Dimension* (London: Routledge & Kegan Paul, 1967).

10. This felicitous phrasing is drawn from Michael Goldberg, *Theology and Narrative* (Nashville: Abingdon, 1982), p. 47.

11. See especially John Van Seters, *In Search of History*.

12. White, p. 23.

13. Cf. Brevard Childs, *Myth and Reality in the Old Testament* (Studies in Biblical Theology 27; London: SCM, 1954).

14. Quoted by Hayden White in 'Historicism, History and the Figurative Imagination', *History and Theory*, Beiheft 14 (1975), p. 51.

15. Lloyd Bitzer, 'The Rhetorical Situation'.

16. See especially his *Metahistory* (Baltimore: Johns Hopkins University Press, 1973).

Notes to Chapter 4

1. For example, James Barr, *Old and New in Interpretation* (New York: Harper and Row, 1966), and Thomas L. Thompson, *The Historicity of the Patriarchal Narrative* (BZAW 133; Berlin: Alfred Töpelmann, 1974).

2. *The Eclipse of Biblical Narrative*, p. 13.

3. These are scattered throughout Biblical legal material. Exod. 18.21-23; 20.16; 23.1-3, 6-8, and so forth. In the ancient Near East, one finds such concerns expressed in places like the epilog of the Code of Hammurabi.

4. *Art of Biblical Narrative*, p. 32.

5. Note the 'best text' principle that is discussed in the Introduction; it is further expounded in 'Finding the Best Job'.

6. *Poetics of Biblical Narrative*, p. 28.

7. *Ibid.*, p. 30.

8. *Institutes of Oratory*, 4.2. 21.

9. In legal contexts, the word 'fact' means the 'deed done' or the 'event that occurred', not the evidence upon which a judgment is based: see H.C. Black, *Black's Law Dictionary* (St. Paul: West, 1968), under 'fact'. This differs from the scientific usage that identifies the facts as the 'givens', and the judgment as to what happened an interpretation.

10. Cf. Deut. 19.18.

11. The apologetic character of this narrative was recognized by Artur Weiser decades ago: 'Die Legitimation des Königs David: zur Eigenart and Entstehung der sogen. Geschichte von Davids Aufstieg', in *Vetus Testamentum* 16 (1966), pp. 325-54. Subsequently Hittite parallels have been suggested by Harry A. Hoffner, in 'Propaganda and Political Justification in Hittite

Historiography', *Unity and Diversity: Essays in the History, Literature and Religion of the Ancient Near East*, ed. H. Goedicke and J.J.M. Roberts (Baltimore: Johns Hopkins, 1975), pp. 49-62. See P. Kyle McCarter, 'The Apology of David', *Journal of Biblical Literature* 99/4 (1980), pp. 489-504, for a sound presentation of the case.

12. 1 Sam. 24; 26; most commentators would ascribe these accounts to different sources, but they are so similar that one could make the case that an account has been 'doubled' for emphasis. The feeding of the five and four thousand in Mark might be offered as an analogy.

13. This account is found in 1 Samuel 27 and 29: David justifies his 'escape to the land of the Philistines', and then engineers an arrangement that allows him to act surreptitiously in behalf of his countrymen. He avoids having to fight with the Philistines against Israel because Achish's colleagues doubt David's loyalty; David uses the opportunity to strike another blow for Judah. Even while David is in a compromising situation, the narrative portrays him as doing for the people of God what a good king would be doing.

14. Many scholars separate 2 Sam. 7 from the narrative of the rise of David; McCarter (*JBL* 99/4 [1980], pp. 490-92) ends the 'rise of David' in 2 Sam. 5.10. However the pattern of forensic narration argues for the divine word in ch. 7 as the conclusion. The problem of this view is that ch. 7 as it now reads shows evidence of Deuteronomistic revision.

15. On this verse, see E.T. Mullen, 'The Royal Dynastic Grant to Jehu and the Structure of the Book of Kings', *Journal of Biblical Literature* 107/2 (1988), pp. 193-206. There are probably many other narratives which can be understood as shaped by apologetic concerns of this sort. For example, the palace coup that toppled the last of the Omrides, Queen Athaliah, appears to be told to justify Jehoiada's deeds in behalf of Jehoash (2 Kgs 11). Athaliah came to the throne by filial murder, demonstrating just how demonic and unnatural was her will to power. The way the coup is arranged demonstrates that the people supported it, and the spontaneous destruction of the temple of Baal and slaughter of its priest manifests the reforming zeal of the parties involved.

16. Note, for example, the title of the article of Keith W. Whitelam: 'The Symbols of Power: Aspects of Royal Propoganda in the United Monarchy', *Biblical Archaeologist* (Sept. 1986), pp. 166-73.

17. Note the views of James C. VanderKam, in 'Davidic Complicity in the Deaths of Abner and Eshbaal: A Historical and Redactional Study', *Journal of Biblical Literature* 97/4 (1980), pp. 166-73.

18. The trajectory from strict forensic narration to this literary extension of it can be traced through a transitional form. In a number of legal narratives in the Pentateuch, the narrator tells the story rather than quoting the *narratio* of the plaintiff or defendant. The account of the origin of the law of blasphemy in Lev. 24.13-16 is preceded by the story of the case which

purportedly called it into being (vv. 10-12). The purpose seems to be to provide the authoritative forensic narration, rather than the potentially flawed one of the interested parties.

19. This list is taken from Westermann, *Basic Forms of Prophetic Speech* (Philadelphia: Westminster, 1967), p. 137. He lists other examples of the judgment of the individual in the history books, but some appear to be Deuteronomistic imitations of prophecy, and others do not confirm very precisely to the form. In the prophetic books, prophecies of judgment against individuals begin to appear without narrative frameworks, e.g., Isa. 22.15-25; Jer. 22.10-12, 13-19, 14-27, 30. But some retain narratives with forensic force, e.g., Isa. 7.1-17; Jer. 20.1-6; 28.12-16; 29.21-23, 24-32.

20. See Westermann, *ibid.*, pp. 129-36; Klaus Koch, in *The Growth of the Biblical Tradition* (New York: Charles Scribner's Sons, 1969), pp. 191-94, objects to the judicial model, preferring 'indication of the situation' to accusation and 'prediction of disaster' to judgment. One wonders what is gained by denying the legal character of the transaction. We prefer 'indictment' over accusation because YHWH's charges are indisputable in principle; I also prefer the more judicial term 'sentence' for the declaration of what YHWH declares will be done.

21. So Westermann, *ibid.*, pp. 133-34.

22. *Poetics*, pp. 154ff.

23. There is good reason to believe that Ahab was a relatively popular king during his lifetime; there are even hints that Elijah was not an implacable foe, e.g., 1 Kgs 18.41-46. It was probably Jehu, who was representative of a rather extreme loyalist position, that established the extremely negative view of Ahab.

24. 2 Kgs 1.2-4, if separated from the man-of-God legend in vv. 5ff.

25. See Dale Patrick's *Rendering of God in the Old Testament* (Philadelphia: Fortress, 1981).

26. See Chapter 1.

27. To be sure, there are critics who dismember the account: e.g. Reinhold Bohlen, *Der Fall Nabot: Form, Hintergrund and Werdegang einer alttestament-lichen Erzählung (1 Kön 21)* (Trierer Theologische Studien 35; Trier: Paulinus, 1978), sets a core narrative apart from the prophetic word, and even from other scenes of the story. The approach here is just the opposite to Bohlen's: Start with the whole and question only those words in it that are clearly out of place. In 1 Kgs 21, only vv. 20-26 seem incongruent; perhaps vv. 27-29 are secondary as well.

28. See the commentaries for the discussion of what was involved, e.g., John Gray, *I & II Kings* (Old Testament Library; Philadelphia: Westminster, 1963), p. 391.

29. Verses 20-24 would appear to belong to the Deuteronomistic Historian, referring to events he has covered previously and will cover subsequently. Moreover, Ahab in these verses is an implacable foe of Elijah and totally

Rhetoric and Biblical Interpretation

unrepentant, a view of him which grew up in later times, expressed by the Dtr. narrator in vv. 25-26. The account of Ahab's repentance in vv. 27-29 is more sympathetic toward Ahab, more or less consistent with his character in 21.1-16. It assumes, by the way, that Ahab died a peaceful death, contradicting 1 Kgs 22. It alludes to Jehu's bloody overthrow of the dynasty a decade later. The paradox is that 1 Kgs 21.27-29 has a more sympathetic view of Ahab than one would expect the dynasty of Jehu to exhibit. This argues against 1 Kgs 21 being created as an apologia for Jehu.

30. This, of course, depends upon what one decides about vv. 27-29; see previous note.

31. Alter, *Art*, pp. 15-16, and Sternberg, *Poetics*, pp. 190-222.

32. Sternberg, *ibid.*, on the way the author leaves gaps for the reader to fill in about how much Uriah knew.

33. Nathan's clever parable reinforces the persuasive power of the divine judgment, not only for David but also for the reader.

34. See McCarter, 'Plots, True or False, The Succession Narrative as Court Apologetic', *Interpretation* 35 (1981), pp. 355-67, for a discussion of the different source divisions.

35. Solomon exiles or eliminates Adonijah, Joab and Abiathar in 1 Kgs 2; the latter two have been woven into previous chapters as leitmotifs. A case has been built up against Joab throughout 1 Samuel; Abiathar's fate is determined by his descent from the accursed house of Eli (1 Sam. 2.31-33 alludes to Abiathar).

36. Sternberg, *ibid.*, pp. 482-515. The other account of Samuel's condemnation of Saul (1 Sam. 13.8-15) leaves the reader uneasy. Although it demonstrates that Saul is guilty as charged, the offense seems vastly disproportionate to the severity of the sentence. Samuel seems to be testing Saul's subservience to prophetic authority, and Saul makes an effort to comply. The reader has not been fully convinced by the forensic narration that YHWH has been just, or at least compassionately just.

37. This designation will be used for the work isolated by Martin Noth in his *Überlieferungsgeschichtliche Studien* (Tübingen: Max Niemeyer, 1957); it runs from Deuteronomy through Joshua, Judges, 1-2 Samuel to 1-2 Kings.

38. This list is taken from G. von Rad, *Studies in Deuteronomy* (Studies in Biblical Theology 9; London: SCM, 1953), pp. 87-88.

39. Variations on this formula can be found in 1 Kgs 15.25-26, 34; 16.12-13, 19, 25, 30-34, etc.; Jehu actually avoids this condemnation, and only is reprimanded for continuing to use Jeroboam's idolatrous cult centers (2 Kgs 10.29, 31).

40. In addition to the passages we put forth as candidates for forensic narration, he incorporated other kinds of prophetic traditions, e.g., 1 Kgs 11.26-40; (16.1-4); 17.1-19.21; 22.1-36, etc. 1 Kgs 16.1-4 is a standard announcement of judgment against an individual, but its wording suggests

that Dtr. formulated it; probably all that was known of Jehu ben Hanani's prophecy was that it had been against Baasha.

41. The thesis put forward by Claus Westermann (*Basic Forms*, pp. 169-76), that the prophecy of judgment against the people is a development of the prophecy of judgment against an individual and that Amos and Hosea are to be credited with first collectivizing the addressee, still seems compelling.

42. Although it was noted earlier that judgments against individuals embedded in narratives are found in the Latter Prophets as well as 1-2 Samuel and 1-2 Kings, in the rest of this section we will concentrate on their place in the latter.

43. Notice the theme, 'what persons will say when they see the ruins' in Deut. 29.22-28; this is one further bit of evidence that the author addressees an audience which is looking back on the disaster.

44. See G.E. Wright, 'The Lawsuit of God: A Form-Critical Study of Deuteronomy 32', in *Israel's Prophetic Heritage: Essays in Honor of James Muilenburg*, ed. Bernard W. Anderson and Walter Harrelson (New York: Harper and Brothers, 1962), pp. 27-67.

45. Psalms 78, 106.

46. We would suggest that at a minimum the following passages fit the description: Amos 2.6-16; (3.1-2; 9.7-8); Hos. 9.10-14; 10.1-2; 11-15; 11.1-7 (or 9); 13.1-3, 4-8; Isa. 1.1-3; Jer. 2.1-13; (3.6-13); Ezek. 16; 20; (23).

47. See Westermann, *Basic Forms*, pp. 182-83; he terms this development of prophecy the 'contrast motif'.

48. The only prophet of communal judgment rendered is Isaiah, and his prophecies are directed to Assyria, not Israel (2 Kgs 19.20-37). 2 Kgs 20.1-19 does have several quasi-prophecies directed to Hezekiah, not, however, prophecies of judgment.

49. Frank M. Cross, 'The Themes of the Book of Kings and the Structure of the Deuteronomistic History', in *Canaanite Myth and Hebrew Epic* (Cambridge, Mass.: Harvard University, 1973), pp. 274-89, argues for two authors of the work, one from the time of Josiah, the other an updating from the exile. If this were the case, the author from Josiah's reign would also be speaking from before the event. We have ignored this possibility because the extant work makes sense without reference to different editions.

50. Though some may have been living in the land of Palestine.

51. Many scholars have recognized this rhetorical purpose in Dtr. This leads us to caution that the conscious use of rhetorical concepts is not going to revolutionize all aspects of Biblical interpretation; at times it will simply confirm what has been recognized before.

52. See, for example, Eliezer Berkovits, *Faith after the Holocaust* (New York: Ktav, 1973), pp. 86, 120-23, 152-59.

53. See Patrick's *Rendering of God*, pp. 108-12.

54. See George Coats, *Rebellion in the Wilderness* (Nashville: Abingdon, 1968).

Notes to Chapter 5

1. Cited by Michael Walzer, *Exodus and Revolution*, p. 8.
2. *The Dimensions of Job* (New York: Schocken, 1969), p. 287.
3. *Ibid.*
4. *Ibid.*, p. 288.
5. *Ibid.*
6. *Ibid.*
7. See Gadamer, *Truth and Method*, pp. 273f., for the argument that there must be a 'fusion of horizons' of the text and the interpreter in order for the interpreter to gain an understanding of the text.
8. Gadamer (*ibid.*, p. 331) advocates strengthening the text, 'for in this process what is said is continually transformed into the uttermost possibilities of its rightness and truth. . . '
9. 'How Law is Like Literature', in *A Matter of Principle* (Cambridge, Mass.: Harvard University, 1985), p. 149.
10. Dworkin on Agatha Christie novels: 'An interpretive style will also be sensitive to the interpreter's opinions about coherence or integrity in art. An interpretaton cannot make a work of art more distinguished if it makes a large part of the text irrelevant, or much of the incident accidental, or a great part of the trope or style unintegrated and answering only to independent standards of fine writing. So it does not follow, from the aesthetic hypothesis, that because a philosophical novel is aesthetically more valuable than a mystery story, an Agatha Christie novel is really a treatise on the meaning of death. This interpretation fails not only because an Agatha Christie, taken to be a tract on death, is a poor tract less valuable than a good mystery, but because the interpretation makes the novel a shambles. All but one or two sentences would be irrelevant to the supposed theme; and the organization, style, and figures would be appropriate not to a philosophical novel but to an entirely different genre' (*A Matter of Principle*, pp. 150f.). One finds all of our criteria used in this quotation.
11. The deconstructionists may be right that all works have gaps and inconsistencies, but one ought not to approach the work bent on showing that to be the case. One should first seek the consistency or unity of the work, and only conclude that there are flaws after a conscientious attempt to find what makes it hang together.
12. We would have to qualify this statement somewhat: The text should be available to a competent, serious reader. Such a reader would not have the expertise to be able to use scholarly classifications, but they would understand the text in the way the classification would expect. Probably the primary role of scholarship is to understand the transactions which have taken place and are taking place between the text and its readers; only secondarily does it create the possibility of new transactions.
13. The theory that a text means what an author intended has been

thoroughly criticized in hermeneutical literature. See Dworkin, *A Matter of Principle*, pp. 154-58.

14. See James Barr, *Comparative Philology*.

15. Translation into another language is a paradigm of any act of making sense of a passage.

16. See *Dimensions*, pp. 16-24.

17. According to Westermann, *The Structure of the Book of Job* (Philadelphia: Fortress, 1981), pp. 139-48; numerous commentators find a distinctive viewpoint in Elihu: so, e.g., Habel, *The Book of Job* (Philadelphia: Westminster, 1985), pp. 36-37, 440-516.

18. Stated most forcefully by Childs, *Introduction to the Old Testament as Scripture* (Philadelphia: Fortress, 1979), pp. 526-44.

19. Cf. Whedbee, 'The Comedy of Job', and Schökel, 'Toward a Dramatic Reading of the Book of Job', in *Semeia 7: Studies in the Book of Job*, pp. 1-39 and 45-61 respectively; a similar strategy is followed by Greenberg, 'Job', in *The Literary Guide to the Bible* (Cambridge, Mass.: Harvard University, 1987), pp. 283-304.

20. Taken from logic: a syllogism which requires another premise to be valid.

21. A point made forcefully by Sternberg, *The Poetics of Biblical Narrative*, pp. 186-90, *et passim*.

22. Cf. Alter, *The Art of Biblical Narrative*, pp. 131-54.

23. As advocates of the 'reconstructionist' strategy, we do recognize the obligation to attribute as much of the extant text to the original as is feasible; in other words, we opt for a 'conservative' reconstructionist strategy. The ready recourse to the classification of 'secondary' by interpreters such as Baumgärtel (*Der Hiobdialog: Aufriss und Deutung* [BWANT 61; Stuttgart, 1933]) is to be eschewed.

24. A list of its distinctive features would include: (1) It is not history or history-like, but a story of occurrences in an unspecified time and far away place. (2) One might associate the story with the stories of primeval times (cf. Ezek. 14f.), but the setting is within the world of nations. (3) Stylistically the narrative is striking for its use of formulaic repetition, a feature reminiscent of ancient Near East myth and epic. (4) The story told is didactic, a kind of hypothetical case teaching a lesson about true piety. (5) It is the most polytheistic story in the Old Testament.

25. For example, Kallen, *The Book of Job as a Greek Tragedy* (New York, 1918); Sewall, *The Vision of Tragedy* (New Haven: Yale, 1956), pp. 1-24.

26. One must keep in mind that a parallel is a scholarly hypothesis, not a fact. To recognize two texts as parallel, the scholar must understand each sufficiently well to identify the respects in which they are similar.

27. An Akkadian text given that title by the translator, Robert H. Pfeiffer, in *Ancient Near Eastern Texts* (Princeton: Princeton University, 1955), pp. 438-40.

28. A Sumerian text given that title by the translator, S.N. Kramer, in *ibid.*, Suppl. Vol. (1968), pp. 589-91.

29. The whole of Westermann's *Structure of the Book of Job* is devoted to identifying the generic features of the constituent parts of the dramatic poem; on the lamentation of Job, see Patrick's refinement of Westermann: 'Job's Address of God', *ZAW* 92/2 (1979), pp. 268-82. There are those, e.g., Habel (*The Book of Job*, pp. 42-43), who have insisted that the poet is only using psalmic language, evidenced by the fact that it is essentially different in purpose and spirit from its normal usage.

30. The author may have a heavy emotional investment in the language of lament, but he has transferred it to the hypothetical world of imaginary literature.

31. See the works by Westermann and Patrick, cited in note 29.

32. For example, Pope's translation of Job 38.2, *Job* (Anchor Bible 15; Garden City: Doubleday, 1965), pp. 249-50; Kraeling, 'A Theodicy and More', *Dimensions*, pp. 210-12.

33. For example, Murray, 'Beyond Good and Evil', and Greenberg, 'In Dust and Ashes', in *Dimensions*, pp. 196 and 224 respectively.

34. For example, Otto, 'The Element of the Mysterious', and Chesterton, 'Man is Most Comforted by Paradoxes', in *Dimensions*, pp. 225-28 and 228-37 respectively.

35. For example, Terrien, *Job: Poet of Existence* (Indianapolis & New York: Bobbs Merrill, 1957), pp. 218-49; Rowley, 'The Intellectual Versus the Spiritual Solution', *Dimensions*, pp. 125-26; Gordis, *The Book of God and Man*, p. 133; and Fohrer, *Das Buch Hiob* (Gütersloh, 1963), pp. 535-36.

36. For example, Curtis, 'On Job's Response to Yahweh', *JBL* 98 (1979), pp. 499-501; cf. Elie Wiesel, *Messengers of God*, pp. 233-34.

37. One might conclude that the answer simply is not satisfactory, but that would belie its dramatic power and grandeur.

38. Richter, *Studien zu Hiob: Der Aufbau des Hiobbuches, dargestellt an den Gattungen des Rechtslebens* (Theol. Arbeiten 11; 1959), argues that the entire work should be construed as a judicial contest. That, however, can only be a metaphor for the action, whereas lamentation is an actual form of transaction with God. That is, Job draws upon judicial language to sharpen his lament.

39. *Dimensions*, pp. 16-24.

40. For example, Gordis, 'The Temptation of Job—Tradition versus Experience in Religion', and Peake, 'Job's Victory', in *Dimensions*, pp. 74-85 and 197-202 respectively.

41. For example, Buber, 'A God who Hides His Face', and Ragaz, 'God Himself is the Answer', *Dimensions*, pp. 56-65 and 128-30 respectively.

42. Cf. Westermann, *Structure*, pp. 105-108.

43. See Dale Patrick's 'The Translation of Job XLII 6', *VT* 26 (1976), pp. 369-71; Morrow, 'Consolation, Rejection, and Repentance in Job 42.6', *JBL* 105/2 (1986), pp. 211-25.

44. Note that we only said 'better'; a better one yet may be advanced, or one already among us may prove more compelling. We can never be sure that we have grasped the text as the best text it can be; that is a transcendent aspiration.

45. See Muilenburg, 'Form Criticism and Beyond'.

46. It reminds one of the first scenes of King Lear.

47. Von Rad, *Old Testament Theology*, I, p. 411, suggests that the work is neutral regarding the respective stances of Job and his companions. We find that unconvincing.

48. Lecture XXXIII; it is published in *Dimensions*, pp. 132-40.

49. *Ibid.*, pp. 134-35.

50. *Ibid.*, p. 135.

51. *Ibid.*, p. 136.

52. *Ibid.*, p. 140. It is a weak negative, for Lowth lamely defends it as an expression of a less developed dramaturgy than that found in Greek tragedy.

53. Westermann, *Structure*, pp. 81-95.

54. See Dale Patrick's *ZAW* article cited in note 29.

55. Westermann, *Structure*, pp. 27-28, proposes that ch. 23 be introduced by 27.5-6; such an address would be a fitting conclusion to the dialog. The material in chs. 24-27 he identifies as fragments and finds homes for them in the first cycle.

56. For example, Pope's in *Job*, pp. 158-74; the solution adopted by Greenberg ('Job', *Literary Guide*, p. 293, drawn from Skehan, 'Strophic Patterns in the Book of Job', *CBQ* 23 [1961], p. 141), that suggests that Job parodies his opponents is too clever, evidenced by the fact that neither ancient nor modern readers have caught it.

57. Most interpreters have in fact assumed that it does, or intends to, whether they discern action in the dialog or not. Note that we have skipped over Job's concluding lament and Elihu's diatribe (chs. 32-37); this was for the sake of simplicity.

58. Morrow, 'Consolation, Rejection, and Repentance in Job 42.6', *JBL* 105/2 (1986), pp. 211-25.

59. *Ibid.*, p. 224.

60. *Ibid.*, p. 225.

61. Note C.H. Dodd's definition of parable: 'At its simplest the parable is a metaphor or simile drawn from nature or common life, arresting the hearer by its vividness or strangeness, and leaving the mind in sufficient doubt about its precise application to tease it into active thought' (*The Parables of the Kingdom*, p. 16).

62. Morrow, *op. cit.*, considers three leading translations/interpretations.

63. The very fact that hitherto he has been prolix and here laconic indicates a profound change.

Notes to Chapter 6

1. An earlier version of this essay, written by Allen Scult with Michael Calvin McGee and J. Kenneth Kuntz, was published in the *Quarterly Journal of Speech*, May, 1986. The present authors express appreciation to Professors McGee and Kuntz and to the editors of the *Quarterly Journal of Speech* for permission to include the essay in this volume.

2. See H. Goldhammer and Edward A. Shils, 'Types of Power and Status', *American Journal of Sociology* 45 (1939), pp. 171-82; Gustav Ichheiser, *Appearances and Realities* (San Francisco: Jossey-Bass, 1970); Alvin W. Gouldner, *The Future of Intellectuals and the Rise of the New Class* (New York: Seabury Press, 1979), pp. 28-47; Renate Mayntz, ed., *Theodor Geiger on Social Order and Mass Society* (trans. Robert E. Peck; Chicago: University of Chicago Press, 1969), pp. 132-65; Louis Althusser, *Lenin and Philosophy and Other Essays* (trans. Ben Brewster; 1966-70; Eng. trans. New York: Monthly Review Press, 1971), pp. 127-86; Karl Mannheim, *Essays on Sociology and Social Psychology* (London: Routledge & Kegan Paul, 1953), pp. 74-153; Helmut Dubiel, *Theory and Politics* (trans. Benjamin Gregg 1978: Eng. trans. Cambridge, Mass.: The MIT Press, 1985); Anthony Giddens, *Central Problems in Social Theory* (Berkeley: University of California Press, 1979), esp. pp. 9-48, 145-50; Paul Ricoeur, *Time and Narrative* (1983; Eng. trans. Chicago: University of Chicago Press, 1984); and Jürgen Habermas, *Theorie des kommunikativen Handelns* (2 vols.; Frankfurt am Main: Suhrkamp, 1981).

The line of thinking that results in a discourse-centered conception of power begins in defining power as complex sociopsychological inducements to action or inaction (e.g., see Goldhammer and Shils). In Ichheiser's tale, power was originally the 'biopsychological superiority of the individual'. As societies grew larger and more complex, there was a double shift in the bases of power: (1) The individual's physical strength came to be less significant than his or her mental cleverness, and, at the same time (2) the personal power of individuals became less significant than 'socially acquired and transmitted indirect means of power'. Concomitantly, there was a shift in moral standards applicable to power: Overt physical types of coercion were stigmatized, while society increasingly pretended that 'psychological and indirect' power did not exist or was in some way 'legitimate' (pp. 136-38). Effective power was thus increasingly invisible.

The social theorist, being an active promoter of what Alvin Gouldner called 'the culture of critical discourse', made a professional obligation out of 'telling the truth' about power. In the past, sociologists have favored a *situation-centered* account of the relationship between truth and power. 'Telling the truth' about power consisted of demonstrating that the truth-claim of an 'ideological' proposition is actually a power-claim that functions to obscure perceptions of 'objective reality' (Geiger, pp. 132-65). Discourse

was portrayed either as 'scientific' (hence 'truthful) or as a determined product of the political economy (of Althusser's 'ideological state apparatus', for example).

Another alternative, now more fashionable, is *discourse-centered*: Anti-positivists (e.g., Mannheim) claimed that even scientific theories (the 'truths' that social theorists tell about power) are power-claims that function to alter or reproduce the conditions of a 'social reality'. 'Telling the truth' about power thus requires an accounting of the social integration of 'truth' and 'power'. As Giddens argues, this entails a more sophisticated understanding of the relationship between discourse and reality. Whether conceived as 'objective' or as 'social', reality is itself a cultural product, perhaps a 'text' (Ricoeur), maybe an elaborate 'speech-act' (Habermas), most certainly a discursively constituted phenomenon obedient to the principles of text-construction. Both truth and power (as well as their opposites) are thus *features of discourse*, objective or material only if discourse is conceived as (semiotically) objective or (historically) material. To theorize power, we must show how discourse *consists of* an integrated power/truth.

3. Alasdair MacIntyre, *After Virtue*, p. 201.

4. Walter R. Fisher develops this idea quite fully in his landmark essay, 'Narration as a Human Communication Paradigm: The Case of Public Moral Argument', *Communication Monographs* 51 (1984), pp. 1-22. See also Walter R. Fisher, 'The Narrative Paradigm: An Elaboration', *Communication Monographs* 52 (1985), pp. 347-67.

5.   See Allan Megill, *Prophets of Extremity: Nietzsche, Heidegger, Foucault, Derrida* (Berkeley: University of California Press, 1985); Clifford Geertz, 'Ideology as a Cultural System', in David Apter, ed., *Ideology and Discontent* (New York: Free Press, 1964); Roland Barthes, S/Z (trans. Richard Miller, 1970; Eng. trans. New York: Hill and Wang, 1974). In traditional usages, as Megill notes (p. 2), the 'aesthetic perspective' would emphasize the priority of 'a self-contained realm of aesthetic objects and sensations' over a 'real world' of nonaesthetic objects'. One major theme of post-modernism, however, is an 'attempt to expand the aesthetic to embrace the whole of reality'. As evinced in the work of such seminal thinkers as Michel Foucault and Jacques Derrida, 'aestheticism' is 'a tendency to see "art" or "language" or "discourse" or "text" as constituting the primary realm of human experience'. Social scientists who turn to discourse analysis (e.g. Geertz) treat 'the real world' as if it were a text in need of aesthetic critique, and literary critics who turn to 'the real world' (e.g. Barthes) treat literary texts as if aesthetic representations capture all significant realities. Megill sees a changing of 'ironies': 'The irony that pervaded modernism tried to uncover a Man or Culture or Nature or History underlying the flux of surface experience. In post-modernism, this has given way to a new irony, one that holds these erstwhile realities to be textual fictions. We are seen as cut off from 'things' and confined to a confrontation with 'words' alone' (p. 2).

6. Perhaps the most influential contemporary work on the Bible as narrative art is Robert Alter, *The Art of Biblical Narrative*.

7. Kenneth Burke begins his 'logological' study of religious discourse with a similar observation regarding the relationship between religious scriptures and persuasion: 'Religious cosmogonies are designed, in the last analysis, as exceptionally thoroughgoing modes of persuasion', *The Rhetoric of Religion: Studies in Logology* (Berkeley: University of California Press, 1961), p. v. See also Allen Scult, 'The Rhetoric of the Pentateuch: An Analysis of the Argument for the Hebrew Concept of God' (Diss. University of Wisconsin-Madison, 1975), for an analysis of the Pentateuch considered as persuasive discourse.

8. Northrop Frye, *The Great Code*, p. 29.

9. The influential medieval commentator Rashi begins his commentary on Genesis by asking this very question. See *The Pentateuch with Rashi's Commentary* (London: Shapiro, Vallentine, 1946), p. 2.

10. See, for example, E.A. Speiser, *Genesis* (The Anchor Bible; Garden City, N.Y.: Doubleday, 1964), pp. xxii-xxxvii; Bruce Vawter, *On Genesis: A New Reading* (Garden City, N.Y.: Doubleday, 1977), pp. 15-24; and especially, Claus Westermann, *Genesis 1–11* (trans. John J. Scullion; Minneapolis: Augsburg, 1984), pp. 569-600.

11. While one finds occasional evocations of such formulas, they appear to be merely vestigial conventions of language shorn of any mythical context that would give them power in and of themselves. For an examination of the use of such mythical language in the Bible, see Yehezkel Kaufmann, *The Religion of Israel, from its Beginnings to the Babylonian Exile* (trans. Moshe Greenberg; Chicago: University of Chicago Press, 1960), pp. 60-121.

12. Gerhard von Rad identifies the two most influential 'core histories' in Deut. 6.20-24 and 26.5b-9 as 'historical creeds' 'The Problem of the Hexateuch'.

13. While one might assume that this power is granted to the text by the 'believer', it might be more accurate to identify the power of sacredness as a rhetorical function of a particular relationship between text and auditor. See Allen Scult, 'The Relationship between Rhetoric and Hermeneutics Reconsidered', *Central States Speech Journal* 34 (1983), pp. 221-28. Michael McGee has another view. He conceives of sacred power as growing out of a perception of structural isomorphism between a sacred narrative and the story that might be told about present life circumstances. See his analysis of Judges 19–21 in 'Secular Humanism: A Radical Reading of 'Culture Industry' Productions', *Critical Studies in Mass Communication* 1 (1984), pp. 1-33.

14. This translation is suggested by E.A. Speiser's characterization of J's image of the relationship between God and Adam at this point as father to small child. See Speiser, p. xxvii. The actual translation does not appear in the book, but was offered by Speiser in a graduate seminar on Genesis, University of Pennsylvania, Fall, 1964.

15. Cf. Hannah Arendt, *On Revolution* (1963; emended, New York: Penguin, 1977), pp. 155-60, 178-202; Carl J. Friedrich, *Tradition and Authority* (London: Pall Mall, 1972), esp. p. 48; and Jürgen Habermas, 'Hannah Arendt's Communications Concept of Power', *Social Research* 44 (1077), pp. 3-24.

16. See Isa. 55.8, where the deity is portrayed as saying, 'For my thoughts are not your thoughts, neither are your ways my ways'; similarly, Hos. 11.9, 'I am God and not man, the Holy One in your midst'.

17. The contrast may be seen in the Babylonian account of creation, *Enuma Elish*, in James B. Pritchard, ed., *Ancient Near Eastern Texts Relating to the Old Testament*, pp. 60-72.

18. Since Fisher's synthesis of social-theoretical work on narrative (Fisher, 1984, 1985), a number of rhetoricians have attempted to accommodate the essentially aesthetic concept 'narrative' with the more pragmatic rhetorical concept 'argument'. Michael McGee has argued for the 're-creation' of argumentation as 'the art of moral reasoning', featuring narrative as a logical operation: 'Particular cases that require moral judgment must be "translated" into the cultural patterns of those charged to judge. The vehicle of translation is *narratio*, a story that structures facts according to the expectations of "native speakers" of a particular culture. . . *Narratio* is to moral reason what the equation is to mathematics, the syllogism to dialectic, and the enthymeme to Aristotelian rhetoric-it is the discourse structure that is uniquely capable of signifying [human conduct]' (pp. 51-53) (Michael Calvin McGee, 'The Moral Problem of *Argumentum per Argumentum*' and 'Recreating a Rhetorical View of Narrative: Adam Smith in Conversation with Quintilian', in J. Robert Cox, Malcolm O. Sillers, and Gregg B. Walker, eds., *Argument and Social Practice: Proceeding of the Fourth SCA/AFA Conference on Argumentation* [Annandale, VA: Speech Communication Association, 1985], pp. 1-15, 45-56).

19. Walter Benjamin, *Illuminations* (ed. Hannah Arendt; trans. Harry Zohn; New York: Schocken, 1969), p. 25.

20. James Stuart (King James VI of Scotland, James I of England), 'The State of the Monarchy and the Divine Right of Kings', speech at Whitehall, 21 March 1609, in *British Oration from Ethelbert to Churchill* (London: J.M. Dent, 1960), p. 18.

21. Giddens, *Central Problems*, p. 149.

22. See Niklas Luhmann, 'Generalized Media and the Problem of Contingence', in J. Loubser, R. Baum, A. Effrat, and V. Lidz, eds., *Exploration in Theory in Social Science: Essays in Honor of Talcott Parsons* (New York: John Wiley, 1979).

23. Elizabeth Tudor (Queen Elizabeth I of England), 'Speech of the Queen', 30 November 1601; in Carl Stephenson and Frederick George Marcham, trans. and eds., *Sources of English Constitutional History* (New York: Harper & Row, 1937), p. 376.

24. Michel Foucault, *The History of Sexuality: An Introduction* (trans. Robert Hurley; 1976; Eng. trans. New York: Random House, 1978). See also Jacques Lacan, *Feminine Sexuality* (ed. Juliet Mitchell and Jacqueline Rose; trans. Jacqueline Rose; 1966-75; Eng. trans. New York: W.W. Norton, 1982), pp. 137-48; Michael Calvin McGee, 'The Origins of "Liberty": A Feminization of Power', *Communication Monographs* 47 (1980), pp. 23-45; and Michael Calvin McGee, *On Feminized Power* (The Van Zelst Lecture in Communication; Evanston, IL: Northwestern University School of Speech, 1986).

Notes to Chapter 7

1. *Old Testament Theology*, I (Philadelphia: Westminster, 1968), p. 520.
2. Volume I was devoted the 'central' covenant, YHWH and Israel, and Volume II to the others.
3. In Patrick's study, 'The Kingdom of God in the Old Testament', in *The Kingdom of God in 20th-Century Interpretation*, ed. Willis, Wendel; (Peabody: Hendrickson, 1987), pp. 67-80, one synthetic concept is experimented with in the way described here.
4. This is the argument of Patrick's *Rendering of God in the Old Testament*.
5. Northrop Frye (*The Great Code: The Bible and Literature*, p. xiii) notes that the Bible despite its appearance of being a small library 'has traditionally been read as a unity, and has influenced Western imaginaton as a unity'.
6. *Canon and Community* (Philadelphia: Fortress, 1984), p. 37.
7. See Chapter 6, 'Genesis and Power: An Analysis of the Biblical Story of Creation'.
8. See Bernhard Anderson's 'From Analysis to Synthesis: The Interpretation of Genesis 1-11', *Journal of Biblical Literature* 97/1 (March, 1978), pp. 23-29.
9. See Meir Sternberg's discussion of repetition, 'The Structure of Repetition: Strategies of Informational Redundancy', *The Poetics of Biblical Narrative*, pp. 365-440.
10. See Brevard Childs, 'The Canonical Shape of the Prophetic Literature', *Interpretation* 32/2 (January 1978), pp. 46-55.
11. We interpret Elihu to be the voice of an offended reader; having this last say, the views of the community, or the wisdom teachers at least, were re-established after their 'defeat' in the dialog. Undoubtedly this facilitated the admission of the work into the canon.
12. See the article cited in note 9 and Childs, *Introduction to the Old Testament as Scripture* (Philadelphia: Fortress, 1979).
13. See the symposium in *Journal for the Study of the Old Testament* 16 (1980).

14. See *Rendering of God*, pp. 137-40.

15. *Sinai and Zion* (Minneapolis: Winston, 1985), p. 213.

16. This is a different question from whether ancient Israel as an empirical community was monotheistic. We agree with those who see the Bible as the product of one 'party' within the national community.

17. Since we cannot reconstruct every author's thought in its entirety, one could even question this very minimal agreement.

18. Note the phrasing of Deut. 13.7: "Let us go and serve other gods', which neither you nor your fathers have known. . .' Since the people obviously did 'know' of these other deities, we must interpret 'know' here as 'recognized as legitimate'.

19. James Boyd White, in *Heracles' Bow: Essays on the Rhetoric and Poetics of the Law* (Madison: University of Wisconsin, 1985), p. 77.

20. See Chapter 6; also *Rendering of God*, pp. 16-18.

21. See *Biblical Interpretation in Ancient Israel*.

22. The reference here is to the movement associated with *JSOT* and its editors, David J.A. Clines, David M. Gunn, and Philip R. Davies, various students of James Muilenburg, et al. Recently literary critics have entered the ranks, particularly Robert Alter and Meir Sternberg.

23. That is how we would characterize Sternberg's views; see *Poetics*, pp. 7-23.

24. That is in fact partly realized in David Clines's *The Theme of the Pentateuch*.

25. The work by John Goldingay, *Theological Diversity and the Authority of the Old Testament* (Grand Rapids: Eerdmans, 1987) is recommended on the means of synthesis.

26. Terrence Fretheim, *The Suffering of God* (Philadelphia: Fortress, 1984), p. 19. Though this sounds plausible, it would require a careful, thorough study of the history of interpretation to confirm.

27. *Book of Common Worship* (Presbyterian Church in the USA, 1946), p. 227.

28. Our ancestors would be able to understand such a view of scriptural revelation. It has its roots in the traditions we share. Indeed, one wonders at their inability to recognize that the doctrine, theology and practice of the religious communities is infected with the same creatureliness and sinfulness as the rest of human activity.

29. See 'Finding the Best Job', Chapter 5 above.

SELECT BIBLIOGRAPHY

Books

Alter, Robert, *The Art of Biblical Narrative*, New York: Basic Books, 1981.

Anderson, Bernard W., and Harrison, Walter, *Israel's Prophetic Heritage: Essays in Honor of James Muilenburg*, New York: Harper and Brothers, 1962.

Aristotle, *Rhetoric*, trans. Lans Cooper; New York: Appleton-Century-Crofts, 1932.

Burke, Kenneth, *Rhetoric of Religion*, Berkeley: University of California, 1961.

—*The Rhetoric of Motives*, Berkeley: University of California, 1969.

Childs, Brevard, *Introduction to the Old Testament as Scripture*, Philadelphia: Fortress, 1979.

Clines, David, *The Theme of the Pentateuch*, JSOT 10; Sheffield, 1982.

Dodd, C.H., *The Parables of the Kingdom*, London: Collins, 1961.

Dworkin, Ronald, *A Matter of Principle*, Cambridge, Mass.: Harvard University Press, 1985.

Eichrodt, Walther, *Old Testament Theology*, I, trans. J.A. Baker; Philadelphia: Westminster, 1968.

Fishbane, Michael, *Biblical Interpretation in Ancient Israel*, Oxford: Clarendon, 1985.

Fisher, Walter R., *Human Communication as Narration: Towards a Philosophy of Reason, Value, and Action*, Columbia: University of South Carolina, 1987.

Frei, Hans, *The Eclipse of Biblical Narrative*, New Haven: Yale University, 1974

Fretheim, Terrence, *The Suffering of God*, Overtures to Biblical Theology; Philadelphia: Fortress, 1984.

Frye, Northrop, *The Great Code: The Bible and Literature*, New York and London: Harcourt, Brace, Jovanovich, 1982.

Gadamer, Hans-Georg, *Truth and Method*, trans. Ganet Barden and John Cunningham; New York: Continuum, 1975; Crossroad, 1986.

—*Philosophical Hermeneutics*, trans. and ed. David Linge, Berkeley: University of California Press, 1976.

Glatzer, Nahum, *The Dimensions of Job*, New York: Schocken, 1969.

Goldberg, Michael, *Theology and Narrative*, Nashville: Abingdon, 1982.

Goldingay, John, *Theological Diversity and the Authority of the Old Testament*, Grand Rapids: Eerdmans, 1987.

Habel, Norman, *The Book of Job*, Old Testament Library, Philadelphia: Westminster, 1985.

Handleman, Susan A., *The Slayers of Moses: The Emergence of Rabbinic Interpretation in Modern Literary Theory*, Albany: State University of New York, 1982.

Hirsch, E.D., *Validity in Interpretation*, New Haven: Yale University, 1967.

Kaufmann, Yehezkel, *The Religion of Israel from its Beginnings to the Babylonian Exile*, trans. Moshe Greenberg; Chicago: University of Chicago, 1960.

162   *Rhetoric and Biblical Interpretation*

Kennedy, George, *Classical Rhetoric and its Christian and Secular Tradition from Ancient to Modern Times*, Chapel Hill: University of North Carolina, 1980.

—*New Testament Interpretation through Rhetorical Criticism*, Chapel Hill: University of North Carolina, 1984.

Levenson, Jon, *Sinai and Zion*, Minneapolis: Winston, 1985.

MacIntyre, Alasdair, *After Virtue*, Notre Dame: University of Notre Dame, 1981.

Mueller-Vollmer, Kurt, ed., *The Hermeneutics Reader*, New York: Continuum, 1985.

Patrick, Dale, *The Rendering of God in the Old Testament*, Overtures to Biblical Theology; Philadelphia: Fortress, 1981.

Pope, Marvin, *Job*, Anchor Bible 15; Garden City: Doubleday, 1965.

Rad, Gerhard von, *Old Testament Theology*, I, trans. D.M.G. Stalker; Edinburgh & London: Oliver & Boyd, 1962.

—*The Problem of the Hexateuch and Other Essays*, London: Oliver and Boyd, 1966.

Rorty, Richard, *Philosophy and the Mirror of Nature*, Princeton: Princeton University, 1979.

Sanders, James A., *Canon and Community*, Philadelphia: Fortress, 1984.

Speiser, E.A., *Genesis*, The Anchor Bible; Garden City: Doubleday, 1964.

Sternberg, Meir, *The Poetics of Biblical Narrative*, Bloomington: Indiana University, 1985.

Suleiman, Susan, *Authoritarian Fictions*, New York: Columbia University, 1983.

Van Seters, John, *In Search of History*, New Haven: Yale University, 1983.

Walzer, Michael, *Exodus and Revolution*, New York: Basic Books, 1985.

Westermann, Claus, *Basic Forms of Prophetic Speech*, Philadelphia: Westminster, 1967.

—*The Structure of the Book of Job*, Philadelphia: Fortress, 1981.

White, James Boyd, *Heracles' Bow: Essays on the Rhetoric and Poetics of the Law*, Madison: University of Wisconsin, 1985.

Articles

Anderson, Bernhard 'From Analysis to Synthesis: The Interpretation of Genesis 1–11', *Journal of Biblical Literature* 97/1 (March, 1978), pp. 23-29.

Bitzer, Lloyd, 'The Rhetorical Situation', *Philosophy and Rhetoric* 1 (1968), pp. 1-14.

Childs, Brevard, 'The Canonical Shape of the Prophetic Literature', *Interpretation* 32/2 (1978), pp. 46-55.

Fischel, Henry, 'Story and History: Observations on Greco-Roman Rhetoric and Pharisaism', in Henry Fischel ed., *Essays in Greco-Roman and Related Talmudic Literature*, New York: Ktav, 1977, pp. 443-72.

Greenberg, Moshe, 'Job', in *The Literary Guide to the Bible*, ed. Alter, Robert and Frank Kermode; Cambridge Mass.: Harvard University, 1987, pp. 283-304.

Morrow, Robert, 'Consolation, Rejection, and Repentance in Job 42:6', *JBL* 105/2 (1986), pp. 211-25.

Muilenburg, James, 'Form Criticism and Beyond', *JBL* 88/1 (1969), pp. 1-18.

Patrick, Dale, 'The Translation of Job XLII 6', *VT* 26 (1976), pp. 369-71.

—'Job's Address of God', *ZAW* 92/2 (1979), pp. 268-82.

—'The Kingdom of God in the Old Testament', in *The Kingdom of God in 20th-Century Interpretation*, ed. Wendel Willis; Peabody: Hendrickson, 1987, pp. 67-80.

Scott, Robert L, 'On Viewing Rhetoric as Epistimic', *Central States Speech Journal* 18 (1967), pp 9-17.

Scult, Allen, 'The Relationship between Rhetoric and Hermeneutics Reconsidered', *Central States Speech Journal* 34 (1983), pp. 221-28.
—McGee, Michael C; Kuntz, J. Kenneth, 'Genesis and Power: An Analysis of the Biblical Story of Creation', *Quarterly Journal of Speech* 72 (1986), pp. 113-31.
Skehan, Patrick, 'Strophic Patterns in the Book of Job', *CBQ* 23 (1961), p. 141.
White, Hayden, 'The Value of Narrativity in the Representation of Reality', in W.T.J. Mitchell, ed., *On Narrative*, Chicago: University of Chicago, 1981, pp. 1-23.

Texts

Pritchard, James B., ed., *Ancient Near Eastern Texts*, Princeton: Princeton University, 1955.
Tanakh: A New Translation of the Holy Scriptures According to the Traditional Hebrew Text, Philadelphia: Jewish Publication Society, 1985.

INDEXES

INDEX OF BIBLICAL REFERENCES

Genesis
1–3	27, 104–106, 119-22, 125
1–2	131
1.1–2a	111
1	33, 34, 134
1.3	107
1.16-18	112
1.31	112
2–3	33
2	33, 34, 134
2.4a	117
2.4b-7	106
3.9	108
3.17ff.	34
3.21	108
5–9	131
6–9	117
12	105, 131
15.13-14	35
20	131
26	131

Exodus
3–4	131
10.1-2	35
13.9	144n16
18.21-23	145n3
20.2	143n12
20.16	145n3
20.22–23.19	61
21.28-32	61
23.1-3	145n3
23.6-8	145n3

Leviticus
17.26	61
24.10-12	147n18
24.13-16	146n18
36.2-4	62

Numbers
27.3-4	62

Deuteronomy
4.32-35	35
6.6-7	39
6.20-25	46
6.20-24	156n12
6.20-21	39
10.21–11.1	36
13.7	159n18
19.18	145n10
26.5-10	46, 47
26.5b-9	156n12
29–30	77
29.1–30.10	76
29.22-28	149n43
30.1ff.	77
32.34-43	77
32	76

Joshua
23	76
24	76
19–21	156n13

1 Samuel
2.12-17	65
2.22-25	65
2.27-36	65
7–12	131
8–2 Sam. 5	72
13.8-15	65, 148n36
15	71
15.1-33	65

16–2 Sam.
7	63
16.1-13	72
24	146n12
26	146n12
27	146n13
29	146n13

2 Samuel
3.36ff.	64
5.1-3	64
5.10	146n14
7	64, 146n14
11–12	65, 70
12.11-12	71
13.20	70
14.4-7	62

1 Kings
1–2	70
2	148n35
9.4	73
11.4	73
11.6	73
11.26-40	148n40
11.33	73
14.8	73
15.3	73
15.5	73
15.11	73
15.25-26	148n39
15.34	148n39
16.1-4	148n40
16.12-13	148n39
16.19	148n39
16.25	148n39
16.30-34	148n39
17.1–19.21	148n40
18.41-46	147n23

1 Kings (cont.)
20.26-43	65
21	68, 148n29
21.1-29	65
21.1-16	148n29
21.20-26	147n27
21.20-24	69, 147n29
21.25-26	148n29
21.25	74
21.27-29	69, 147n27, 148nn29,30
22	148n29
22.1-36	148n40

2 Kings
1.2-4	65, 147n24
1.5ff.	147n24
9-10	63, 64, 72
9.25-26	64, 69
9.36-37	64, 69
10.10	64
10.17	64
10.29	148n39
10.30	64
10.31	148n39
11	146n15
14.3	73
116.2	73
17	76
17.7-23	75
17.19-20	77
18.3	73
19.20-37	149n48
20.1-19	149n48
22.2	73
24-25	77

Job
1-2	89
1.22	89
2-3	97

3-23	99
3	89
6-7	93
9-10	93
12-14	93
13	99
13.16	100
15-16	94
17	99
18	94
19	99
20	94
21	94
22	94, 99
23	153n55
23-28	90
24-28	99
24-27	153n55
24	94, 99
27.5-6	153n55
28	90
29-31	94
32-37	153n57
32.2-3	100
33-37	90
38.1-42.6	97
38.2	152n32
40.8	100
42.2-6	100
42.6	97
42.7-17	97
42.7ff.	89
42.7	95

Psalms
78	149n45
106	149n45

Isaiah
1.1-3	149n46
7.1-17	147n19

22.15-25	147n19
55.8	157n16

Jeremiah
2.1-13	149n46
3.1-4.4	142n19
3.6-13	149n46
20.1-6	147n19
22.10-12	147n19
22.13-19	147n19
22.14-27	147n19
22.30	147n19
28.12-16	147n19
29.24-32	147n19
29.21-23	147n19

Ezekiel
14f.	151n24
16	149n46
20	149n46
23	149n46

Hosea
9.10-14	149n46
10.1-2	149n46
10.11-15	149n46
11.1-9	149n46
11.1-7	149n46
11.9	157n16
13.1-3	149n46
13.4-8	149n46

Amos
2.6-16	149n46
3.1-2	149n46
7.10-17	65
9.7-8	149n46

INDEX OF AUTHORS

Alter, R. 18, 50, 58, 59, 142nn23,24,
    143n13, 145nn7,4, 148n31, 151n22,
    156n6, 159n22
Althusser, L. 154n2, 155n2
Anderson, B.W. 158n8
Arendt, H. 21, 157n15
Arnold, M. 44, 144n27
Auerbach, E. 39

Barr, J. 145n1, 151n14
Barthes, R. 155n5
Baumgärtel 151n23
Beiner, R. 142nn27,28
Benjamin, W. 120, 157n19
Berkovits, E. 149n52
Bitzer, L. 34, 143n11, 145n15
Black, H.C. 145n9
Bohlen, R. 147n27
Buber 152n41
Burke, K. 13, 49, 142nn9,17, 144n5,
    156n7

Chesterton 152n34
Childs, B. 13, 142n20, 145n13, 151n18,
    158nn10,12
Clines, D. 159n24
Coats, G. 149n54
Cross, F.M. 149n49
Curtis 152n36

Derrida, J. 155n5
Dodd, C.H. 153n61
Dubiel, H. 154n2
Dworkin, R. 21, 84, 142n29, 150nn9,10,
    151n13

Eichrodt, W. 127, 128, 158nn1,2

Fischel, H. 143n6, 144n20
Fishbane, M. 135, 159n21
Fisher, W.R. 144n6, 155n4, 157n18

Fohrer, G. 152n35
Foucault, M. 123, 155n5, 158n24
Frei, H. 45, 46, 57, 144n1, 145n2
Fretheim, T. 159n26
Friedrich, C.J. 157n15
Frye, N. 104, 142n21, 156n8, 158n5

Gadamer, H.G. 12, 16, 42, 141nn1,6,
    142nn18,19,26, 144nn19,22, 150
    nn7,8
Geertz, C. 155n5
Geiger 154n2
Giddens, A. 154n2, 155n2, 157n21
Glatzer, N. 82, 84, 150nn2,3,4,5,6, 151n16,
    152n39
Goldberg, M. 145n10
Goldhammer, H. 154n2
Goldingay, J. 159n25
Gordis, R. 152nn35,40
Gouldner, A.W. 154n2
Gray, J. 147n28
Greenberg, M. 151n19, 152n33, 153n56
Gunkel, H. 16

Habel, N. 151n17, 152n29
Habermas, J. 154n2, 155n2, 157n15
Handleman, S.A. 144nn17,18
Hirsch, E.D. 42, 144n23
Hoffner, H.A. 145n11
Huizinga, J. 51

Ichheiser, G. 154n2

Kadushin, M. 144n26
Kallen 151n25
Kant 21
Kaufmann, Y. 156n11
Kennedy, G. 29, 31, 141n4, 143nn1,2,6
Koch, K. 147n20
Kraeling 152n32
Kuntz, J.K. 143n31, 154n1

Lacan, J. 158n24
Levenson, J. 132, 135, 159n15
Lévi-Strauss 54
Linge, D. 144n19
Lowth, R. 98, 99, 153nn48,49,50,51,52
Luhmann, N. 123 157n22

MacIntyre, A. 43, 103, 144nn24,25, 155n3
Mannheim, K. 154n2, 155n2
McCarter, P. Kyle 146nn11,14, 148n34
McGee, M.C. 143n21, 154n1, 156n13, 157n18, 158n24
Megill, A. 155n5
Morrow, R. 152n43, 153nn58,59,60,62
Muilenburg, J. 11-18, 23, 24, 27, 141 nn1,2,3, 142nn10,11,12,13,14,15,16,19, 143n5, 153n45, 159n22
Mullen, E.T. 146n15
Murray 152n33

Noth, M. 148n37

Otto, R. 152n34

Parsons 123
Patrick, D. 147n53, 152nn29,31,43, 153n54, 158nn3,4, 159nn14,20
Peake, A.S. 152n40
Polanyi, M. 145n9
Pope, M. 152n32, 153n56

Rad, G. von 135, 144n3, 148n38, 153n47, 156n12
Ragaz 152n41
Richter 152n38
Ricoeur, P. 142n26, 154n2, 155n2
Rivkin, E. 144n21
Rorty, R. 12

Rowley, H.H. 152n35

Sanders, J. 130, 131, 158n6
Schleiermacher 142n18
Schökel, L. Alonso 151n19
Scott, R.L. 1411n7
Scult, A. 143n31, 154n1, 156nn7,13
Seters, J. van 145nn8,11
Sewall 151n25
Shils, E.A. 154n2
Skehan, P. 153n56
Speiser, E.A. 143n10, 156nn10,14
Sternberg, M. 18, 19, 59, 67, 71, 72, 142nn22,25, 145nn6,7, 147n22, 148 nn31,32,36, 151n21, 158nn9,12, 159nn22,23
Suleiman, S. 47, 144n4

Terrien 152n35
Thompson, T.L. 145n1

VanderKam, J.C. 146n17
Vawter, B. 156n9

Walzer, M. 142n21, 150n1
Weber, M. 123
Weiser, A. 145n11
Westermann, C. 93, 147nn19,20,21, 149 nn41,47, 151n17, 152nn29,31,42, 153nn53,55, 156n10
Whedbee 151n19
White, H. 36, 46, 53, 54, 143nn14,15, 144n2, 145nn12,14,16
White, J. Boyd 134, 159n19
Whitelam, K.W. 146n16
Wiesel, E. 152n36
Wright, G.E. 149n44

INDEX OF SUBJECTS

Apologetic, 72-373
    political, 72-73
    theological, 66-67, 71-72, 75-78
Augustine of Hippo, 29-30
Aristotle, 12, 21, 47
Audience, as construed by historical
    and fictional narrative, 48-49
    narrative appeal to, 108-109
    rhetorical exchange with, 17, 19-
        21, 22, 23, 25, 26, 73-75, 77-
        78, 81-83, 86-87, 88, 95-96

'Best text' criterion, 21,-23, 25, 26, 27,
        84-87, 88-96, 97, 98, 101-102,
        135, 137, 138, 139
    applied to historical narratives, 45-46
    applied to reading of different
        documents, 106

Canonical Criticism, 130-32, 136
Canonical Process, 131-32, 135
Casuistic Law, 61
Cogency, as interpretive criterion, 86-
        87
Coherence, as interpretive criterion, 128,
        137-38
Communal function, 14
Community of interpreters, 22-23
Composite texts, 17
    'P-J' in Genesis, 116-19
Comprehensiveness, as interpretive
    criterion, 85, 90-92, 137
Confirmatio (argument), 61-62, 75-76,
        77
Consistency as interpretive criterion,
        85-86, 91-92
Covenant, 76, 128
Creation narratives, comparison with
    Mesopotamian mythologies, 33
    Priestly account, 33, 111-16
    Yahwist account, 106-11
Critical Interpretation, 130-31, 136

David and Bathsheba, 70-71
David's Rise to Power, 63-64
Descriptive Praise, 93
Deuteronomistic History, 73-78
Dialectic of power, 122-24
'Dialog about Human Misery', 92
Disputation, 193

Enuma Elish, 32, 37-38
Evolutionary Schemes, 128-29, 135-36
Exile, 77-79
    and hope, 77-79
    and repentance, 77-79
Exodus from Egypt, rhetorical meaning
        of, 34-36
Exodus narratives, status as history, 45

Fiction, 25-26, 57-59
Forensic Narration, 25, 60-64, 65-71,
        74-75
    as an analogy, 63-64, 75
    in defense, 63-64
    in prosecution, 65-71, 73-75
Form and Content, 14-15, 18
Form Criticism, 11-12, 13-16

God, rhetorical motive of, 31-36
    rhetorical function of acts in history,
        34-36
    power of, as characterized by 'J', 110-
        11
    as characterized by 'P', 115-17

Hermeneutics, 14, 19-21, 22
    and Rabbinic literature, 40, 42
    hermeneutical circle, 22, 24
History, rhetorical view of, 25, 57-60,
        79
    God's rhetorical use of, 34-36
    and fiction, 37, 45-53
    and fact, 58-60, 63, 66, 69, 71, 78-
        79

rhetorical manipulation of, 59-60
Homer, 39

Ideal Reader, 16, 18-20, 23-24, 129,
        132, 134, 136-38, 139
Ideology of Kingship, 66-67, 73-75
Interpretation, as rhetoric, 22
        Bible's prescription for, 39-40
        criteria for, 21-22, 25, 83-84, 85-
                87, 139
        'best text' criterion, 21-23, 25, 26,
                27, 84-87, 88-96, 97, 98, 101,
                135, 137, 138, 139
        'best text' applied to historical
                narratives, 45-46
                applied to reading of different
                        documents, 106
        interpreter's roles, 23-24
        interpretive freedom, 137-39
Invention, 54-55

Jehu's Rebellion, 64, 69
Job, 81-102
        translation, 88-89
        sources, 89-92
        Elihu, 90, 100
        original vs. extant text, 91-92
        genre, 92-96
        dramatic resolution, 94-95, 99-102
        dramatic structure, 97-102
        dramatic poetry, 93, 97, 98-99
        prose narrative, 93, 97

Lament, 93-94, 95, 96, 102
Law, rhetorical character of, 34-36
Literary Approach, 17-19, 135-36

Magic, and rhetoric, 38
'Man and His God', 93
Mesopotamian epics, contrast with Biblical
        prose narrative, 32ff., 37
Monotheism, 133, 136-39

Naboth's Vineyard, 68-69
Narratio, 61-62, 63, 114
Narrative, artistry of, 17, 18, 50, 66-67,
        104
        as persuasion, 25-26
        rhetorical nature of, 36-38
        contrast with the epic, 37-38
        and Rabbinic Midrash, 40-41

contrasted with Greek philosophy, 41
as history, 45-46
realistic, 46
fable, 47
as constitutive of Jewish community,
        50-51
and truth, 104, 109
and power, 110
'narrative logic', 110-12

Origen, 29

Passover Seder, rhetorical significance
        of, 38, 52
Philosophy, Greek, contrasted with
        Biblical narrative, 40-41
Plenitude, as interpretive criterion, 87,
        94
Pluralism, in the OT, 128-39
Power, discourse-centered theory of, 104-
        105
        God's, as authorship, 117
        as authority, 118
        dialectic of authorship and authority,
                119-20
Priestly Writer ('P'), 112-17
Precritical interpretation, 128, 130, 135
        levelling the text, 135
Profoundity, as interpretive criterion,
        87, 94, 97
Prophecies of judgment against individuals,
        66, 68
        in narratives, 65-67
Propaganda, 64

Quintillian, 61

Rabbinic Literature and rhetoric, 30f.,
        40-43
        and contemporary hermeneutics,
                40, 42
        Midrash and Biblical prose narrative,
                41
Religious communities, 22-23, 136-37
Rhetoric, 12-13
        distinction between primary and
                secondary, 29
        and Rabbinic literature, 30, 31
        Biblical narrative as, 31-35
        as characterization of divine activity,
                31-35

rhetorical situation, 34, 54
rhetorical constitution of covenant
    community, 35-36 52-53
and magic, 38
and 'truth', 46
Rhetorical, significance of Passover Seder,
    38, 52
'identification', 49-53, 109
character of Biblical history, 51-53
conventions, 55
situation, 34, 54
style of Yahwist, 107-23
style of Priestly writer, 112-19
Rhetorical Criticism, 11-13, 14, 16-18,
    20-21, 24, 27, 30, 136, 139

Sacred text, rhetorical power of, 107
Sitz im Leben, 14, 25
Source Criticism, 14, 17, 20
Synthesis, in OT theology, 27, 129,
    131-39

Text as living discourse, 14-16, 20, 23
Theodicy, 93-95
Theology, 130, 133, 137
Throne Succession Narrative, 70-71
Tradition History, 135
Tree of Knowledge, 106, 108
Truth, and rhetoric, 46
    claims of historical narratives, 50-
        51, 53-55
    and power, 104
    and narrative, 104-105, 109

Unity of OT teaching, 128-29, 136-38
Universal in particular, 67, 72-78

Will to Power, 103, 105
Wisdom, 93-95

Yahwist ('J'), 106-11